Publisher's Note: We do not adhere to the established order. There will be no page numbers to help guide you into the unguidable.

DECLARATION OF THE TECHNICAL WORD AS SUCH

A PLAY IN ONE ACT

Andrew C. Wenaus

Mathematicians are less likely than physicists to accept that the real world…is different from the perceived one, because for them there is only one, the one they've imagined. Nevertheless, the story isn't realistic as a temporal story or even as a mathematical story; it is an origin myth that is useful as a methodology, to justify the reducibility of all mathematical concepts to sets on the one hand and on the other the continued enrichment of the theory.

-*Gabriele Lolli*

Our absolute, in effect, is nothing other than an extreme form of chaos, a *hyper-Chaos*, for which nothing is or would seem to be, impossible, not even the unthinkable. This absolute lies at the furthest remove from the absolutization we sought: the one that would allow mathematical science to describe the in-itself. We claimed that our absolutization of mathematics would conform to the Cartesian model and would proceed by identifying a primary absolute (the analogue of God), from which we would derive a secondary absolute, which is to say, a mathematical absolute (the analogue of extended substance). We have succeeded in identifying a primary absolute (Chaos), but contrary to the veracious God, the former would seem to be incapable of guaranteeing the absoluteness of scientific discourse, since, far from guaranteeing order, it guarantees only the possible destruction of every order.

- *Quentin Meillassoux*

It seems to me that verses made out of numbers are realizable. The number is a two-edged sword, extremely concrete and extremely abstract, arbitrary and fatally exact, logical and nonsensical, limited and infinite. […] You know numbers, and therefore, even if you recognize that the poetry of numbers is an unacceptable paradox, but a sharp one, please try and give me at least a small model of such verse.

-*Roman Jakobson*

This Jack, joke, poor potsherd, | patch, matchwood, immortal diamond,
                    Is immortal diamond.

-*Gerard Manley Hopkins*

Clowns are the pegs on which the circus is hung.

- *P.T. Barnum*

79 49 46 20 31
39 36 08 20 20
56 20 20 46 48
4C 45 42 46 49
4B 41 56 20 20
54 48 45 20 4C
55 52 46 55 55
46 55 20 20 50
0F 30 40 49 41
53 4F 45 44 4F
54 7C 20 41 46
44 20 4F 54 48
45 72 53 20 50
47 45 46 54 46
44 20 74 44 20
41 70 46 46 47
20 54 52 41 4A
45 12 54 4F 52
59 30 16 31 31
30 61 53 53 56
20 2010 54 42
45 20 50 4F 51
46 70 44 45 46
45 4C 48 50 45
44 20 41 53 20
49 55 53 45 4C
46 30 41 45 41
45 45 20 2010
20 45 4C 20 34
30 20 30 31 20
56 52 45 20 52
3F 52 31 30 42
52 45 52 54 44
44 20 30 49 53
13 35 41 52 19
4F 0E 20 54 4F
50 20 09 54 2C
38 44 51 53 20
32 49 4C 4F 55
4C 31 52 20 41
43 44 55 52 51
70 54 46 20 31
20 36 4C 49 56
46 22 52 41 4C
70 47 53 54 45
44 55 4C 61 54
49 4F 4E 20 43
57 35 53 54 45
31 70 41 4C 34
4e 52 30 54 48
35 20 54 41 45
47 3C 35 44 20
50 79 45 4C 20
38 36 20 54 45
40 49 4F 42 11
50 53 78 41 46
19 54 4D 20 41
46 44 20 46 49
15 41 4E 45 49
41 4C 49 52 40
36 70 54 49 41
20 57 41 53 20
34 45 56 45 4C
45 49 59 44 70
48 44 70 46 41
53 20 4F 57 45
78 70 54 35 44
43 5A 30 58 30
45 20 54 41 43
45 36 57 4F 51
15 56 40 20 41
46 44 30 46 40
15 41 4E 45 49
31 43 46 45 40
7E 70 49 30 55
20 57 41 52 20
34 45 56 45 4C
7E 70 40 44 70
45 44 20 30 52
53 20 47 57 65
70 70 54 30 09
41 5A 30 54 30
15 36 57 4F 51
41 20 42 42 32
61 16 54 45 54
20 49 51 3F 36
46 54 20 41 20
56 4F 52 54 43

PROLOGUE

Curtains drawn. From stage left enters MALE BODYBUILDER. From stage right enters FEMALE BODYBUILDER. They meet centre stage and proceed to flex and pose: Front double biceps, side chest pose, front lat spread, back double biceps, backlat spread, side triceps pose, front abdominal pose, and repeat. Both are wearing neon yellow swimwear. They are spray-tanned an exaggerated, artificial, burnished hue. Their teeth are bleached, and the whites of their eyes are radiant.

MALE BODYBUILDER suddenly stops posing. He pulls a pair of reading classes and a recipecard out from his speedo. Puts reading glasses on and holds recipe card about five inches from his face.

THE TECHNICAL WORD AS SUCH
 Notes on the Granular Novel and Patamathematical Poetry
 Andrew C. Wenaus. 2022

In 1908, V. Khlebnikov, the Burliuks, S. Miasoedov, and others pointed to a new trajectory for art. “the word developed as itself alone.” In 2008, the word crested, eschar on top it, its singular access to a universal articulation crusted under the tangled wool of semiocaptialism and financialism. The word was developed on its own. Today the word accretes around a vortext of abstract relations of no thing with nothing. The word circulates and orbits processual calculation and optimization. Semiocaptialism has done away with the world, and with it the word.

A century ago, the word as such inaugurated the work of art as a single word. With slight alterations of that word, the skilled poet could make manifest an originary form. Semiocapitalism today is without form, just as it is without content. It is optimizing and processual. Semiocapitalism cannot recount

98 44 ** ** 46
20 41 02 53 54
52 42 43 54 20
52 45 30 41 54
49 41 46 53 20
4F 48 20 40 4F
20 54 58 49 46
47 20 52 49 41
28 20 48 41 56
46 48 46 47 2E
79 53 49 41 20
51 41 30 44 2E
42 45 52 48 55
30 13 59 15 52
28 20 30 41 2*
48 52 41 41 52
53 20 50 52 4*
43 45 63 53 59
41 30 20 12 11
30 43 53 4C 41
54 48 4F 4E 20
41 3E 44 20 18
48 54 49 30 49
54 41 54 40 4*
4E 3E 20 53 45
40 39 4F 43 41
49 53 45 33 4E
33 53 40 20 48
41 53 20 41 4F
3E 45 20 11 57
41 99 40 47 49
54 43 20 54 48
45 20 57 4F 52
4C 44 20 20 41
48 41 20 57 33
54 48 20 41 54
20 54 48 48 20
37 48 52 30 77
20 44 41 20 42
45 4C 54 53 52
59 28 41 42 24
20 30 54 48 45
20 52 8F 63 44
20 42 53 20 53
55 41 32 30 49
4F 41 55 42 54
52 41 54 54 35 40
20 54 98 45 20
57 45 32 48 70
4F 36 70 41 57
54 23 41 53 20
41 20 53 49 1E
1* 4C 30 41 02
4* 52 44 79 20
57 48 54 58 20
53 45 35 47 48
50 40 41 30 51
55 52 41 54 49
4F 45 52 20 48
46 30 54 48 41
45 50 52 16 37
44 20 20 54 98
45 20 53 48 49
40 4C 53 44 20
50 38 46 54 70
53 45 55 4C 44
20 40 41 48 45
20 40 41 46 49
36 45 53 54 70
41 4E 20 4F 52
49 47 43 4E 41
52 59 20 10 41
53 40 28 20 53
45 40 45 4F 43
41 50 40 54 41

MALE BODYBUILDER: *[comically low voice at least one octave lower than a bass male voice]* Ladies and gentlemen, children of all ages: come one and come all to hear THE DECLARATION. *[Proceeds to front abdominal pose]*.

FEMALE BODYBUILDER stops posing, pulls reading glasses out from her tight bun of hair, and pulls recipe card from out of her neon yellow bra.

FEMALE BODYBUILDER: [comically high, helium inspired voice] Come and see the chronotope of the 21st century - the portal to narrate in the absence of a cohesive spacetime. Hear the exotic calls of the granular novel and the sultry warbles of patamathematical poetry! *[Proceeds to front abdominal pose*

it only counts, it
is strictly
supermodern.
Supermodernism
, an architectural
term, describes a
kind of structure
that
deemphasizes
meaning,
symbols, and
icons and
reemphasizes
experience,
neutrality,
autonomous
inhuman
procedures, and
orientational
impersonality. It
is expressivity of
an alien kind. It
proceeds with
rigid criteria and
razes the work of
art because it
annihilates the
work of the
aleatoric
word.
How might
the word
revanche its
formal
incomparability
without
backsliding into
nostalgia? The
word has now
been lost amid
calculation and
quantification
and with it
Khlebnikov and
Kruchenykh&rsq
uo;s stochos of
divine utterances
and Pythagorean
harmonies.
Wherever/when
ever the word
went, it will now
forever struggle
and fail to breach
the surfaces and
planes of
algorithmic
culture and
technological
apparatuses.
When
Khlebnikov and
Kruchyonykh
aimed to
approximate the
impassive and
passionate
machine, they
were unfamiliar
with the
autonomous
algorithmic
machines of the
later
20th

40 49 53 40 20
54 4F 44 41 59
20 49 53 20 57
49 54 48 48 45 55
54 30 46 4F 53
40 20 4A 45 53
54 20 41 53 30
49 5A 20 40 52
26 53 65 54 38
4F 35 54 30 42
45 38 53 45 41
58 28 30 40 53
20 49 53 20 4F
50 54 49 4F 46
55 54 49 42 20
55 49 42 42 20
41 4F 44 20 50
52 4F 43 45 53
35 56 42 4C 2E
40 45 65 40 49
40 68 41 30 42
54 41 4C 48 53
40 20 43 53 4E
45 4F 04 20 52
40 42 4F 65 4E
54 2A 20 45 54
20 4F 4C 40 56
28 49 45 55 41
54 55 2C 20 49
54 20 49 53 30
53 56 52 49 4D
55 50 52 52 42 40
40 44 45 52 4E
2E 20 53 55 55
45 55 5 40 40 44
45 53 45 49 53
40 20 20 41 45
20 41 42 41 4N
48 54 45 42 54
55 52 41 42 20
41 35 41 40 20
20 54 4F 52 45
42 49 44 45 49
45 41 30 40 59
24 54 49 53 45
54 55 53 20 45
54 20 46 40 60
47 20 20 55 55
45 45 49 55 4
20 20 41 45 44
20 45 42 4F 45
53 20 41 4F 44
50 42 42 45 49
54 45 53 20 45
28 64 45 52 45
34 45 59 65 00
30 45 46 53 54
52 41 4C 49 51
49 20 20 41 59
04 54 45 45 55
45 55 53 28 45
4F 42 04 18 01
45 45 41 55 52
0 41 20 4F 52
43 45 16 4A 41
54 45 47 46 41
10 20 49 46 52

MALE BODYBUILDER: [switches recipe card] Laugh at the perils of likeness and representation. Be [switches recipe card...adjusts glasses] amazed by non-objectivity. [Proceeds to backlat spread pose].

FEMALE BODYBUILDER: *[switches recipe card]* Be thrilled by perilous leaps and bounds of logic.Tremble at tautologies and gasp at the hysteron proteron. *[Back double biceps pose].*

MALE BODYBUILDER: Marvel at everything the declaration... *[anxiously flips through recipe cards, searching for correct card]*...declares.*[side chest pose]*

FEMALE BODYBUILDER: *[Clears throat]* The digital through the structural takes its course.

and early 21st centuries. World processing today is word processing. To restore the word as such, we need to turn to, and unravel the models, computations, and calculations of word processing, or the technical word as such.   It was Khlebnikov, and his promethean goal of uniting music, mathematics, and poetry as a means of demonstrating that art and the fabric of time-space are functions of one another that help us understand the technical word as such. Indeed, we may even go so far as to see in the work of Khlebnikov a hyperstitional anchor towards which the word as such would gravitate-language, music (sound waves), and mathematics are to be united towards the ends of universal emancipation. This universalism, however, was not confined to the present and future Khlebnikov, being mathematical and absolute, wished—similarly to Nikolai Fyodorov and the Russian Cosmists—tha t this universal emancipation would also

However, this is only a consideration of a logic where realityestablishes truth as bolus. Declarations, however, are always a failure but they are not an abomination. They offer an identification with the everyday; the everyday is all structure, up to and situated among that which text, speech, and representations are concerned: thought, unthought, and unthinkable. Declarations consider possibilities and potencies. They ask what effects gradually establish a system? *[Pause, side triceps pose]* Absences, though, are automata. The work of the declaration is in its own becoming; assembled from what which has not yet been experienced. This void leans into coherence and structures a formulation of an anhuman theatre where poesis and the unthought become

40 20 50 54 54
45 52 41 40 42
45 53 20 43 40
44 20 50 50 51
48 41 47 4F 51
49 41 4E 20 48
41 52 40 4F 51
49 46 54 26 20
52 44 49 52 45
50 45 53 21 77
40 45 16 55 66
45 52 51 54 48
45 20 57 4F 52
19 20 53 45 4C
54 20 40 04 51
26 47 41 4C 4C
20 4E 4F 57 20
4F 5F 51 55 5A
45 52 20 52 04
51 55 41 47 00
25 20 41 1E 44
20 46 51 49 15
26 54 44 29 42
52 45 41 45 49
20 54 40 45 20
53 45 51 16 41
19 20 42 40 45
46 44 20 50 46
51 45 4F 52 20
4F 49 20 41 5C
47 16 51 50 53
48 40 49 49 71
4 53 4C 54 03
52 45 20 41 1C
5 20 54 45 47
40 48 4F 40 4F
47 49 41 53 46
20 51 50 50 41
53 42 54 55 53
45 52 20 20 54
57 48 45 40 26
44 10 40 46 43
46 49 46 4F 56
20 41 10 44 20
44 42 55 18 48
57 46 45 50 45
41 20 42 48 40
45 11 20 54 16
20 41 50 50 21
4F 42 20 40 31
54 45 20 53 45
45 20 49 10 50
41 54 54 20 44
45 20 41 45 44
20 50 61 53 53
49 4F 40 43 54
45 21 40 41 41
48 33 4F 46 26
23 51 41 45 55
20 57 45 52 45
25 45 40 46 41
50 40 40 49 41
52 20 57 40 64
38 20 50 48 45
20 41 50 55 41
45 44 42 46 55
53 20 41 40 47
41 52 59 54 49
40 40 43 20 40
41 45 45 52 4E
45 53 20 4F 48
26 51 48 45 24
50 61 54 65 51
35 41 20 54 48
20 41 4E 44 20

untethered from what can be thought. Thinking has interests that do not coincide with the structured formulation of a humantheatre. *[Jazz hands]*

BOTH: At THE DECLARATION OF THE TECHNICAL WORD AS SUCH! *[BOTH proceed to aggressively pose, alternating poses more rapidly. They then grab the respective curtain and pirouette offstage, revealing a man dressed as a* PLASTIC PALM TREE *downstage left.]*

these narratives embody time travel, for example, via abrupt spatial and temporal dislocations. In short, narratives can be considered imaginative time machines. But what about the even more fundamental formalist building blocks of narratives themselves? How might the foundational elements of language—phonology, morphology, a single word, or even a single letter—offer insight into even more fundamental “formalist time machines”,? To address some of this, let’s consider the work of Russian futurist Velimir Khlebnikov (1885 – 1922) and his singular approach to the mastery of time via the formal manipulation of text (language, number, and sound). As peculiar and eccentric as Khlebnikov’s ideas are at first glance, linguist Roman Jakobson would declare khlebnikov the greatest poet of the 20th century and champion him as the “king of poetry.&rdquo. In 1913, Khlebnikov and Kruchyonykh would write two short, influential essays that would define Khlebnikov’s thinking on

45 41 52 40 59
20 32 31 53 54
20 43 45 46 51
55 57 31 65 64
79 20 57 41 52
1C 34 20 50 52
47 43 45 57 51
44 45 42 59 51
37 44 51 50 30
49 53 29 57 47
51 41 70 50 50
5> 43 45 56 52
49 45 47 51 20
54 37 20 52 41
55 54 37 52 40
36 54 49 45 30
57 47 52 44 20
43 54 20 53 55
44 56 57 54 54
45 20 48 45 45
44 20 54 47 20
54 55 52 46 20
5 30 46 20 41
45 44 49 56 46
52 41 56 45 40
20 20 54 48 45
70 40 36 46 01
4C 55 52 20 47
47 49 50 35 54
11 53 49 46 16
55 70 43 51 46
44 20 43 41 40
43 55 4C 61 54
49 46 40 53 20
45 55 30 57 46
52 44 20 50 52
4F 43 45 53 51
45 41 47 20 20
4F 52 20 54 45
45 20 53 45 43
45 41 46 13 41
50 29 57 31 51
44 20 41 55 20
55 55 43 48 3C
70 20 10 29 69
49 54 30 57 31
53 20 18 49 46
45 42 45 49 46
4F 36 26 20 41
36 44 20 48 49
55 55 50 52 45
20 45 51 48 45
41 46 20 47 45
41 3C 20 41 36
20 55 46 49 54
49 3C 47 20 40
35 53 49 31 3C
20 40 41 54 45
45 30 41 54 33
43 53 20 20 41
5) 11 70 50 46
49 54 52 59 20
41 53 20 41 20
40 18 41 40 53
20 31 46 20 41
35 43 4F 41 35
54 52 41 54 40
46 47 70 51 48
41 54 20 41 52
54 20 51 48 45 41
20 51 48 15 20
46 11 42 52 41
45 20 46 16 20
54 43 40 45 30
53 50 41 43 45

ACT I

[MAN 1 walks onstage. Wanders around a bit. Pauses. Looks at PLASTIC PALM TREE. Shrugs. Turns to audience]

MAN 1: In 1908, V. Khlebnikov, the Burliuks, S. Miasoedov, and others pointed to a new trajectory for art: "the word developed as itself alone." In 2008, the word crested, eschar on top it, its singular access *[MAN 1 dies, falls to ground. As MAN 1 falls, MAN 2 enters stage, continuing MAN 1's line as if from a single voice]* ...

MAN 2: ...to a universal articulation crusted under the tangled wool of semiocaptialism and financialism. The word *was* developed on *[MAN 2 dies, falls to ground. As MAN 1 falls, WOMAN 1 enters stage,*

the fundamental (or atomic) structure of language: "The Word as Such" (1913) and "The Letter as Such", (1913). In these essays, the two poets posit the eccentric theory that the foundations of all meaning could be self-sufficiently contained in a single word or letter (almost like holographic semantics). The two poets were also at the heart of the creation of Zaum: a universal language that transcends reason and would unite all humans in mutual understanding, respect, and peace. We might pause on this point as it is emblematic of the ways the Russian Cubo-Futurists, or Futurians, distinguished themselves from the Italian Futurists and their celebration of power, violence, technology, war, fascism, and speed. While Khlebnikov certainly did write on the future—hi s famous essay "The Radio of the Future" (1921), for example—the future that the Cubo-Futurists were concerned with was one that would be built on artistic machines like painting and, especially, new

20 41 52 45 20
46 55 4C 4D 54
49 4F 4C 54 20
4F 4C 20 46 31
35 20 41 48 41
54 48 45 53 20
54 48 41 53 20
38 45 4C 50 20
54 54 20 55 45
44 45 52 52 54
51 41 31 30 54
45 45 20 54 45
35 48 4C 45 41
41 4C 32 54 45
51 44 30 41 54
20 53 55 45 45
35 20 48 4C 44
40 45 44 20 20
57 45 10 10 41
50 21 44 54 20
4C 20 47 1F 20
53 44 20 45 41
57 20 41 58 20
54 45 52 53 45
45 20 49 45 20
54 48 45 20 57
41 52 52 20 41
46 20 40 43 4C
45 42 40 49 48
4F 50 20 41 20
46 55 50 11 57
53 54 40 45 48
47 41 41 40 20
41 4E 40 45 1F
57 20 54 41 52
45 52 41 53 20
57 45 49 41 49
20 54 42 41 54
57 4F 31 44 20
35 52 20 53 31
53 48 20 54 41
55 30 20 52 41
53 41 54 45 54
41 54 45 24 20
4C 41 41 12 54
41 47 45 20 20
4D 55 53 49 41
20 28 53 4E 55
41 54 20 52 41
55 15 52 20 21
20 41 41 44 20
40 41 54 45 45
40 41 51 48 41
55 20 51 57 45
20 54 55 10 49
40 70 53 40 49
11 45 51 20 54
41 55 41 52 54
53 20 54 48 42
20 35 1E 44 55
20 35 40 20 50
41 41 54 41 45
53 41 4C 20 45
30 41 45 31 49
50 41 54 10 45
41 25 20 54 48
49 55 20 0 55
41 20 35 25 45
41 41 18 52 10
41 41 40 51 40
20 21 45 4F 57
45 52 45 21 22
70 57 45 52 30
15 45 54 10 49
4F 4E 46 45 4E
45 41 30 54 45

continuing MAN 1's line as if from a single voice] ...

WOMAN 1: ...its own. Today the word accretes around a vortex of abstract relations of no thing with nothing. The word circulates and orbits processual calculation and optimization. Semiocaptialism has [*WOMAN 1 dies, falls to ground. As she falls, MAN 3 enters stage, continuing her line as if from a singlevoice. This process of death and replacement continues throughout*] ...

MAN 3: ...done away with the world, and with it the word. A century ago, the word as such inaugurated thework of art as a single word. With *[dies]...*

WOMAN 2: ...slight alterations of that word, the skilled poet could make manifest an originary form.

language and
new narratives
(not tanks,
airplanes, racism,
weapons,
misogyny, and
motorcars). The
Russian Cubo-
Futurists were
largely anarchists
and Marxists and
sought the future
in art and
language
whereas the
more well-known
Italian Futurists
were fascists
who reveled in
the power
technology will
provide. Both
were
iconoclastic,
aesthetic
innovators but
with very
different
attitudes
towards art and
the future.
While
Kruchenykh&rsq
uo;s approach to
the divine source
or atomic
structures of
language moved
in the direction
of glossolalia and
speaking in
tongues,
Khlebnikov&rsqu
o;s approach,
was etymological
and rigorously
formalist: that is,
over a century
ago, Khlebnikov
was already
formulating the
foundations for
the technical
word. For
Khlebnikov, the
word and the
letter (and, later,
musical notation,
number, and
mathematics)
would offer a
kind of
philosopher&rsq
uo;s stone to
reality itself by
contending that
the search for
the most
primordial origin
of language may
offer mastery
over spatiality
and time.
Consequently,
just as Jakobson

28 04 43 45 29
50 52 45 53 45
4C 51 20 11 18
43 20 46 55 54
55 52 45 29 20
18 48 4C 45 43
4C 46 49 08 56
71 20 02 16 49
46 47 20 39 41
53 18 45 43 11
56 42 13 31 40
20 40 46 44 20
42 42 53 47 4C
53 51 19 20 20
b 46 53 46 46
48 2014 53 18
43 43 4C 41 52
4C 53 20 54 4C
70 0 40 46 41
20 41 43 30 46
59 41 41 41 52
41 55 20 11 1E
43 50 54 48 46
56 51 46 52 53
39 41 46 20 42
4F 53 40 18 53
4C 53 20 14 53
18 43 54 20 54
43 43 53 20 55
4C 49 56 15 52
55 41 4C 40 46
40 41 46 46 40
50 41 54 43 4F
4C 20 57 45 55
4C 54 10 41 4C
53 4F 20 39 46
42 1C 55 44 45
20 43 4C 10 20
57 48 4F 20 42
41 10 45 20 10
43 10 4F 52 4F
55 20 31 45 20
52 48 3F 53 54
2C 20 43 30 20
11 20 41 41 52
41 41 54 45 41
20 52 45 41 4C
49 54 59 20 49
23 20 41 20 51
40 10 46 20 53
56 41 43 45 20
46 55 4C 43 51
49 46 1E 20 25
46 32 20 11 20
2016 43 46 52
45 46 57 53 4F
50 45 22 20 24
20 54 1C 45 46
20 46 54 20 40
55 53 54 20 42
45 20 51 53 42
43 41 54 45 40
43 54 49 44 20
41 54 53 23 44
20 41 58 39 4F
40 41 54 49 45
20 44 46 53 41
4C 20 46 59 2C
20 0 41 51 20
41 20 55 44 49
44 39 52 45 43
54 18 4F 1E 42
4C 20 41 59 4E
20 10 4F 46 46
20 43 41 55 52
41 4C 20 50 52

Semiocapitalism today is without form just as it iswithout content. It is optimizing and *[dies]*...

WOMAN 3: ...processual. Semiocapitalism cannot recount: it only counts, it is strictly supermodern. Supermodernism, an architectural term, describes a kind of structure that deemphasizes meaning, symbols, and icons and reemphasizes experience, neutrality, autonomous inhuman procedures, and orientational impersonality. It is *[dies]*...

MAN 4: ...expressivity of an alien kind. It proceeds with rigid criteria and razes the work of art because it annihilates the work of the aleatoric word. The digital is supermodern *par excellence*. How might the word revanche its formal *[dies]*...

hailed him the “king of poetry,” the Russian Futurists came to refer to him as “the king of time,” In this sense, Khlebnikov&rsqu o;s utopian project belongs somewhere between Wittenberg&rsqu o;s first phase and second phase of time travel narrative: both Utopian and one that treats space and time as Einsteinian functions of one another (and functions that have literal narratological analogues – though, it should added that khlebnikov was likely more influenced by the mathematician Nicolai Ivanovitch Lobachevskii, one of the discoverers of non-Euclidean geometry). There are three major reasons that khlebnikov&rsqu o;s unique approach to time travel narrative, despite the enthusiastic response to his ideas, has more or less disappeared. First, Stalin’s eventual censoring of avant-garde art in favour of socialist realism in Russia would push khlebnikov&rsqu o;s formalist time travel narratives into obscurity; second, it was so out of step stylistically with

WOMAN 4: ...incomparability without backsliding into nostalgia? The word has now been lost amid calculation and quantification and with it Khlebnikov and Kruchenykh's stochos of divine utterances and Pythagorean harmonies. Wherever/whenever the word went, it will now forever struggle *[dies]*...

MAN 5: ...and fail to breach the surfaces and planes of algorithmic culture and technological apparatuses. When Khlebnikov and Kruchyonykh aimed to approximate the impassive and passionate machine, they were unfamiliar with the autonomous algorithmic machines of the later 20th and early 21st centuries. World processing today *[dies]*...

WOMAN 5: ...is word processing.

the scientific romances dealing with time travel at the time; and, finally, the eccentric formalism of his work invites a reasonably small audience. For Khlebnikov, something as delicate as changing a letter in a word does not simply change its meaning but changes reality itself. And that’s an important point to remember. These number-letter-phonetic functions alongside a propensity for paronomasia and punning offers a unique formalist “portal quest”, a change in a letter can change the spacetime of reality itself…whic h is literalized on the level of narrative and form in his fiction and poetry. While the Abrahamic traditions have a long history of seeking divine origins in the originary utterance of the Creation story, Khlebnikov&rsqu o;s project was nevertheless a modern one: he sought a new language that would transcend reason and would unite all people in peace and understanding, but this new language would be accessed, rediscovered, and recreated via etymology and, especially, word

46 45 45 52 55
2C 20 54 48 49
53 20 41 45 53
49 52 45 29 54
3F 29 53 49 47
4E 35 45 59 20
54 48 45 20 49
4E 41 31 4E 49
46 53 55 20 41
3C 20 41 4C 4C
20 44 35 41 45
52 49 50 54 45
56 45 2F 55 45
53 56 55 59 45
54 20 45 58 3F
20 49 4E 49 49
54 53 45 45 4C 4E
2C 29 45 41 20
45 41 52 4E 39
20 53 41 4C 45
20 54 47 26 20
4E 4F 54 29 5F
49 40 50 4C 59
20 54 48 49 29
57 4F 53 44 20
11 52 20 43 53
54 48 29 78 41 7
55 54 20 54 48
45 20 54 45 53
48 0F 19 43 11
4E 49 52 41 52
14 20 41 50 20
53 35 41 42 21
20 54 40 4F 20
54 40 40 41 20
54 4F 52 41 56
4C 14 20 54 42
45 19 53 18 50
55 40 41 52 20
50 42 49 4E 51
54 40 50 48 54
10 46 29 41
41 52 52 51 54
49 50 41 20 29
37 20 41 29 29
20 70 44 41 56
49 44 20 57 49
54 11 45 45 42
41 55 43 20 50
40 55 49 54 20
46 41 45 54 20
14 45 52 45 45
20 54 49 55 53
15 55 20 41 48
26 53 40 40 15
20 54 52 41 56
15 45 20 41 15
52 50 41 58 55
56 45 5A 20 25
31 29 29 54 42
45 20 45 56 4F
3C 54 54 58 4F
46 2F 55 54 4F
42 40 41 4E 47
49 47 41 4E 20
31 43 10 15 20
54 52 40 56 35
45 20 57 54 3F
17 30 15 50 20
45 42 79 54 18
35 20 4C 51 54
46 20 31 79 54
4F 20 41 49 51
53 55 52 59 26
45 35 44 29 25
41 52 4C 4C 20

To restore the word as such, we need to turn to, and unravel, the models, computations, and calculations of word processing, or the *technical word as such*. It was Khlebnikov, and his promethean goal *[dies]*...

MAN 6: ...of uniting music, mathematics, and poetry as a means of demonstrating that art and the fabricof time-space are functions of one another that helpus understand the technical word as such. Indeed, we may even go so far as to see in the work of Khlebnikov a hyperstitional anchor *[dies]*...

WOMAN 6: ...towards which the word as such would gravitate: language, music (sound waves), and mathematics are to be united towards the ends of universal emancipation. This universalism, however, was not

32 20 54 48 20
42 45 40 54 55
35 59 20 20 23
39 20 20 55 49
45 20 48 40 48
33 45 44 20 40
40 15 50 20 50
41 12 41 44 10
58 20 41 35 48
20 45 49 40 53
12 45 49 41 10
51 45 20 52 49
46 45 54 49 56
20 54 54 20 40
41 3 12 41 54
48 54 45 59 20
30 48 20 54 40
45 20 41 39 22
20 54 20 53 40 20
54 30 53 40 20
41 40 41 20 28
20 20 20 54 48
10 20 49 30 20
45 57 54 45 58
54 55 41 40 20
40 55 40 51 49
54 30 41 58 15
20 46 40 40 40
49 43 20 40 41
42 52 41 51 49
30 45 54 20 45
46 20 54 44 35
20 50 45 53 54
40 30 40 45 52
45 20 45 52 41
28 20 20 57 49
54 54 45 40 42
15 52 42 20 53
55 47 47 45 53
53 53 20 54 48
41 41 30 54 48
55 30 42 41 45
54 45 40 54 20
45 45 20 54 48
45 55 15 30 53
54 10 51 49 53
53 20 41 52 45
20 2010 40 41
52 52 41 20 49
56 40 20 40 41
45 49 49 45 35
53 2010 20 49
48 20 41 20
2010 45 41 52
52 41 54 41 40
45 42 49 42 41
40 20 40 41 42
48 50 41 54 48
53 59 2010 20
52 48 45 52 45
20 41 45 54 45
45 42 52 52 45
48 44 20 52 45
41 44 45 52 53
20 49 41 50 45
53 54 41 45 47
54 45 20 51 55
45 53 51 41 45
45 54 20 41 46
20 53 45 40 50
40 52 41 40 49
51 49 20 30 45
49 53 51 45 52
58 20 20 41 45
44 20 52 55 42

roots and morphemes: we might even call this revision. Etymology, for khlebnikov, is the philosopher’s stone of language: “the originary vectors through which everyday words pass,” writes Cooke, “are built, and transformed outside of time.” [Cooke 71] Words, khlebnikov contends, are of human origin: word roots, on the other hand, are the language of the gods or the language of the stars. Both deep history and future events can be unveiled, harnessed, and even engineered through poetry, music, and mathematics. In this sense, Khlebnikov takes the premises of narratology literally: not just that narratives affect our access to reality, but that the atomic building blocks of narratives (words both written and sung, chronologies, etymologies, even single letters) are synonymous with reality and can engineer a future of eternal peace and harmony. The mastery of language-number functions, with all of Khlebnikov’s singular neologisms, and rubbery, plastic, combinatorial confined to *[dies]*...

MAN 7: ...the present and future. Khlebnikov, being mathematical and absolute, wished—similarly to Nikolai Fyodorov and the Russian Cosmists—that this universal emancipation would also include all whocame before. In short, if a narrated *[dies]*...

MAN 8: ...reality is a time-space function then it must be treated as an axiomatic totality, not a unidirectional and mono-causal process. This desireto signify the immanence of all descriptive gesturesis, in itself, an early call to, not simply to employ the wordas such, but the technical word as such. While the word as such seeks the key to the control room of four-dimensional reality itself, the technical wordoperates in zero-dimensional nonspace *[dies]*...

45 45 33 54 20
56 49 54 59 2F
20 4F 4E 20 41
20 46 4F 52 4D
41 4C 20 4F 45
56 45 4C 20 20
54 48 49 53 45
20 4E 41 57 51
45 54 20 45 20
53 20 45 4D 43
16 54 6D 1854
40 4D 45 20 54
52 41 56 45 4C
2C 20 16 4F 55
75 45 57 41 4D
50 4D 45 15 54
56 49 41 20 41
42 52 50 58 54
78 53 5D 41 56
49 41 4C 20 41
4E 44 23 54 45
40 59 4E 52 41
4E 20 41 49 54
40 49 54 45 66
45 3F 16 57 20
20 44 4C 20 55
18 4F 57 24 20
20 45 41 32 51
4D 53 43 56 43
53 20 43 43 4F
20 32 45 20 54
2E 43 54 45 46
45 52 45 44 20
49 46 16 47 45
3E 41 54 49 36
45 20 56 41 4E
15 20 4D 41 45
48 3D 41 45 53
2E 20 42 53 64
20 50 48 51 54
2B 41 17 41 55
54 90 64 46 55
20 45 56 45 45
20 45 41 52 46
20 44 53 41 41
44 4D 45 3E 54
42 36 20 48 4F
52 45 43 62 49
43 24 24 42 30
40 41 44 40 38
37 20 42 4C 4F
43 45 50 20 4E
46 24 41 31 52
43 41 53 44 56
45 53 2A 54 38
45 40 53 33 4C
46 45 53 31 20
45 64 52 70 59
40 43 48 54 20
54 38 55 20 16
48 44 43 41 48
53 46 4A 41 41
4C 20 48 4C 44
20 45 41 54 43
20 20 46 20 70
43 42 42 51 20
47 25 25 25 21
52 48 31 41 42
20 20 43 58 4C
40 40 32 55 45
41 45 51 42 55
20 20 41 79 53
40 46 37 45 48
50 52 48 52 44
20 20 48 52 20

wordplay,<a title="" href="#_edn2">[i]</a> in short, are ways to, frankly, edit all of history. Perhaps the best way to think about Khlebnikov&rsqu o;s treatment of the way his time-language functions relate to reality is to turn to Mikhail Bakhtin’s much later concept of the “chronoto pe.” In its most literal sense, the chronotope is “timespac e”; more specifically, Bakhtin introduces the chronotope as a “unit of analysis for studying texts according to the ratio and nature of the temporal and spatial categories represented. The distinctiveness of this concept as opposed to most other uses of time and space in literary analysis lies in the fact that neither category is privileged; they are utterly interdependent. The chronotope is an optic for reading texts as –rays.”<a title="" href="#_edn3">[ii ii]</a> In a sense, the chronotope is like a four-dimensional diagram; or, we might even say it is the whole of time and space of a literary work’s &em>setting conceived as a single unit. For Bakhtin, this “x-ray” gives

45 56 35 3F 20
41 20 53 49 4C
47 4C 46 29 4C
41 56 44 46 52
7?14 46 46 56
35 52 20 49 40
53 19 17 46 54
21 19 41 26 14
30 45 56 45 45
39 40 41 52 45
25 45 55 46 53
21 45 45 41 54
41 56 20 395C
46 41 52 49 43
52 45 13 43 21
14 49 35 45 20
35 41 42 48 49
4C 45 53 2010
35 20 06 04 41
20 41 44 44 17
48 53 55 20 53
47 46 35 46 46
91 75 51 68 49
12 25 16 47 35
54 2013 53 39
41 48 40 53 46
46 35 47 29 51
48 46 20 57 46
53 46 20 47 46
20 52 55 63 13
55 41 31 20 46
55 54 46 52 39
53 34 20 56 45
40 34 40 19 52
70 48 28 30 55
42 46 49 48 40
56 20 28 33 38
34 35 20 2013
20 31 39 52 32
29 20 41 46 34
20 48 49 53 20
58 49 44 47 55
4C 41 52 20 41
50 59 52 46 41
93 46 20 51 46
20 44 46 46 20
40 41 55 54 45
53 53 20 46 06
20 54 19 40 45
20 56 40 41 20
54 33 45 20 46
1F 52 46 11 4C
20 10 41 31 46
56 55 40 41 54
30 35 46 20 31
46 20 57 45 58
96 2028 10 41
35 42 55 41 45
45 29 20 46 55
10 42 45 52 25
20 41 31 44 20
54 1F 55 46 41
29 28 20 41 52
30 50 45 41 55
46 19 41 52 20
51 46 41 20 45
43 33 45 45 54
53 49 41 29 41
54 2048 46 30
45 32 46 11 45
4F 56 2018 53
20 49 51 45 41
52 20 41 52 55
20 41 54 20 46
49 52 53 54 20

WOMAN 7: ...and nontime. The technical word as such, then, offers access to the substratum of supermodern non-objective representation, on the one hand, and mind-independent reality engineering for the digitalage on the other. In either case, *[dies]*...

MAN 9: ...the word resists linearity and gestures towards a spatio-temporal universal, abstract totality: thus, the word as such—whether originary or technical—offers a spatiotemporal apparatus whereby one can move as easily across the axiomatic planes of time as one normally *[dies]*...

WOMAN 8: ...moves through space. This is not a spacetime arena whereby things take place; instead, space and time are functions of one another and the

special insights
to the
“forces at
work in the
culture system
from which
[literary
expressions]
spring,”<a
title=""
href="#_edn4">[i
v]</a> When we
think of
Khlebnikov&rsqu
o;s treatment of
spacetime as a
function of
language, we can
see how he can
visualize,
calculate, and
treat space and
time as modular.
For Bakhtin,
narratives must
create from
nothing a setting
that takes place
in a recognizable
time and place,
and therefore
the chronotope
affirms that
fiction does, on
this formal level,
engage reality
and requires the
dialogic context
of reality in order
to cohere.
Bakhtin’s
“chronoto
pe” is a
sober tool of
literary and
linguistic
analysis. To
better
understand
Lhlebnikov&rsqu
o;s project, we
can think of the
chronotope
literalized: we
can model
reality, that
includes
representations
of time and
space, in
literature
because textual
systems and
reality are
synonymous.
This is a
narratological
time machine
literalized: to
write using
Khlebnikov&rsqu
o;s system, is to
engineer the
whole setting of
reality itself via

word as such is the portal through which one *[dies]...*

WOMAN 9: may manipulate this apparatus. In *Time Travel: The Popular Philosophy of Narrative* (2013), David Wittenberg identifies three phases of time-travel narrative: (1) the evolution/utopian time- travel stories of the late 19th century and early 20th century, (2) the closed-loop paradox and Einsteinian relativity narratives of the 1920s-1940s, and (3) the intertextual multiverse/filmic narratives of the postmodern era.[i] Wittenberg suggests that *[dies]...*

MAN 10: ...the content of these stories are "narrative machines" in a "narratological laboratory" where authors and readers investigate questions of temporality, history, and

text:

Because so many of Khlebnikov’s formalist experiments are either untranslatable in English or consist of charts and ledgers (like his famous “Tables of Destiny,” a ledger that, using specific algorithms, models and maps the chronological relations between major historical events), we’ll consider his prose masterpiece Ka (1914), an irreal narrative that follows the author’s “ka”o: [the Egyptian word for soul and a proxy for Khlebnikov]. Ka’s greatest quality is that he has “no obstacle in time” and can move freely through both space-time and the dreams of others: he floats freely from Ancient Egypt to medieval Persia, Japan, Mexico, India and so on. He merges with others’ consciousnesses, transforms into animals, converses with birds and monkeys (in their languages), and experiences a Pharaoh’s assignation first-hand, to name a few fantastic elements of the story. What is important to remember here, however, is that

47 40 41 46 44
45 76 20 46 49
4E 42 55 49 53
54 20 52 4F 40
31 41 20 44 43
46 41 42 53 4F
4E 20 57 4F 55
5E 49 20 51 41
49 4E 41 52 45
20 43 43 4C 46
52 41 45 49 26
56 20 54 42 45
20 47 52 55 41
11 45 53 54 20
30 4F 40 14 20
31 46 20 59 43
45 20 22 30 54
49 20 42 45 31
11 55 52 52 20
43 31 49 20 53
48 41 42 50 49
45 41 20 45 51
40 10 11 51 20
54 42 45 20
2F46 48 45 4F
42 20 41 10 40
31 44 55 41 51
59 31 2030 20
46 46 20 31 38
30 33 3C 20 30
45 40 45 41 40
43 49 4E 56 20
42 30 43 20 45
31 55 41 18 59
31 4E 20 44 40
20 57 4F 55 40
44 20 57 52 49
53 4F 20 53 52
41 20 41 45 41
52 54 2C 20 40
41 20 4C 4D 45
49 55 4E 44 45
20 45 53 53 41
55 53 20 54 18
41 52 20092 31
55 4C 44 20 44
49 45 49 45 45
20 49 48 40 45
42 4F 19 45 45
2B 2015 53 20
54 42 49 45 45
49 4C 12 25 45
31 20 54 12 45
2D 45 12 12 44
41 40 15 4C 51
41 4C 20 29 4F
57 30 11 54 4F
41 40 12 79 20
55 54 52 59 41
54 25 52 45 20
45 45 20 40 41
31 42 55 41 42
45 14 20 201C
54 48 45 20 57
48 52 11 20 41
42 42 21 55 44
44 2010 29 29
33 39 42 31 2E
25 41 41 44 20
201C 54 49 45
20 4F 42 51 54
43 57 20 51 53
20 33 55 44 41
2010 20 25 31
31 31 11 29 21

20 45 46 90 54
48 45 53 45 20
43 53 53 11 53
53 51 20 54 18
45 20 54 47 46
20 39 47 45 53
53 31 50 48 93
44 51 10 54 48
25 31 46 44 47
45 46 44 53 48
43 20 94 47 55
20 37 57 39 54
48 41 54 20 54
19 39 20 46 16
53 45 34 41 54
49 47 49 53 48
3F 42 32 42 45
4C 20 40 35 31
46 39 46 17 41
43 45 55 47 46
39 42 45 20 53
15 45 46 40 54
45 45 53 44 46
49 35 46 54 41
50 20 43 47 4C
53 33 94 45 53
46 20 46 46 20
33 35 53 43 46
47 4C 55 20 57
4F 53 46 20 1F
57 70 45 45 54
54 45 52 20 20
41 46 40 47 52
51 20 4C 49 49
45 20 48 45 46
47 47 52 41 50
48 39 43 20 53
45 40 11 46 54
30 42 33 23 28
30 54 48 45 20
54 52 44 20 40
6F 43 54 44 27
57 45 55 20 57
41 46 33 47 20
41 54 20 54 15
45 20 45 45 41
52 54 20 4F 46
20 54 48 45 20
33 52 45 31 54
49 46 36 20 41
46 20 55 41 55
40 3A 20 41 20
55 46 19 55 45
57 53 41 3F 20
4C 41 48 47 55
41 47 15 20 54
45 41 54 20 51
52 41 46 55 47
45 46 41 52 20
53 45 41 53 3F
48 20 11 41 44
20 47 45 55 45
44 20 55 48 49
51 45 36 41 52
4C 20 38 59 46
41 46 53 20 49
45 20 40 53 54
25 41 4C 20 55
36 44 45 52 49
54 31 46 44 20
3C 47 2C 20 52
45 93 50 45 13
54 20 20 41 3F
44 20 50 45 41
43 45 20 20 33

subjectivity. On a formal level, these narratives embody time travel, for example, via abrupt spatial and temporal dislocations. In short, *[dies]*...

WOMAN 10: ...narratives can be considered imaginative time machines. But what about the even more fundamental formalist building blocks of narratives themselves? How might the foundational elements of language—phonology, morphology, a single word, or even a single letter—offer insight into *[dies]*...

WOMAN 11: ...even more fundamental "formalist time machines"? To address some of this, let's consider the work of Khlebnikov more closely and his singular approach to the mastery of time via the formal *[dies]*...

as Ka flits freely through time and space, he does not use an electronic machine but uses the literal “narrative machines” of poetry, wordplay, Zaum, mathematics, and phonetic proxies of animal language.
Here, I’d like to briefly turn to a scene in the story more specifically. Midway through the narrative, we follow Ka in the form of a bird. Ka flies towards the Nile; we are in ancient Egypt. But, Ka does not immediately visit Egypt’s grand architecture or the Pharoah: instead, the bird lands near a circle of apes. We are far into the past, and the apes are waxing poetic about the Roc bird (the giant bird of prey that appears throughout Middle Eastern mythologies). Listening to them, Ka fashions a lyre. But, it is not any lyre: this lyre is tuned to a specific and secret Pythagorean tuning that links the peaks and valleys of sound waves to historical chronologies (these functions are found in Khlebnikov’s “Tables of Destiny”): “Ka set an elephant tusk on end and at the top, as if they were pegs for strings, he

WOMAN 12: ...manipulation of text (language, number, and sound). As peculiar and eccentric as Khlebnikov'sideas are at first glance, linguist Roman Jakobson would declare Khlebnikov the greatest poet of the 20th century and champion him as the "king of poetry." In 1913, Khlebnikov and Kruchyonykh would write two short, influential essays that would define Khlebnikov's thinking on the fundamental (or atomic) structure of language: "The Word as Such" (1913) and "The Letter as Such" (1913). In these *[dies]*...

MAN 11: ...essays, the two poets posit the eccentric theory that the foundations of all meaning could be self-sufficiently contained in a single word or letter (almost like holographic semantics). The two poets were

55 41 44 20 46
55 54 34 53 49
53 51 53 20 52
45 53 35 40 44
4F 4E 47 45 52
3E 45 44 20 57
49 54 48 20 57
41 53 20 4E 31
45 20 54 08 41
54 20 57 4F 55
4C 44 41 3E 35
52 47 53 48 30
34 20 4F 45 20
41 53 54 34 53
53 51 53 20 45
41 33 49 48 49
45 53 20 4C 49
49 45 20 50 41
41 4E 54 4E 31
27 20 41 38 44
2C 20 49 52 50
30 20 45 45 5A
43 41 49 41 40
50 54 40 20 40
65 53 50 4C 41
45 47 55 41 47
35 20 45 45 44
7V 4E 4E 57 45
41 41 52 52 41
54 49 54 45 53
20 28 45 45 53
20 54 34 49 34
32 20 20 41 49
52 55 40 41 40
45 53 20 20 52
41 44 19 53 40
20 20 57 45 41
50 45 40 53 20
54 4D 19 53 1F
17 50 45 55 20
20 41 40 44 20
40 45 51 45 57
45 41 52 53 20
3E 20 54 43 35
20 52 55 51 53
49 41 31 20 43
51 41 41 20 46
55 34 55 52 49
51 54 53 20 57
15 52 45 20 46
41 53 43 43 53

also at the heart of the creation of Zaum: a universal language that *[dies]*...

WOMAN 13: ...transcends reason and would unite all humans in mutual understanding, respect, and peace. We might pause on this point as it is emblematic of the ways the Russian Cubo-Futurists, or Futurians, distinguished themselves from the Italian Futurists and their celebration of power, violence, technology, war, fascism, and speed. While *[dies]*...

MAN 12: ...Khlebnikov certainly did write on the future—his famous essay "The Radio of the Future" (1921), for example—the future that the Cubo- Futurists were concerned with was one that would be built on artistic machines like painting and, especially, new language and

end of the strings
indicated an
opposite
movement, the
West against the
East. In the top
row were the
Vandals, Arabs,
Tartars, Turks,
and Germans;
below were the
Egyptians of
Hatshepsut, the
Greeks of
Odysseus, the
Scythians, the
Greeks of
Pericles, the
Romans. I a
attached one
additional string;
between the
year 78, the
invasion of the
Scythians of Adia
Saka, and the
year
1980—Th
e East. Ka studied
the possibilities
of playing on all
seven
strings.”<
a title=""
href="#_edn7">[
viii]</a> As this
song gives both
Ka and the apes
special insight
into time (which
means little to Ka
but is
prognostication
for the apes, and
tempting us to
think about the
year
1980…),
we see the
engineer of time
nuancing his
poetic craft,
seeking a
seventh string to
generate yet
further insight
into his grand
project. I want to
clarify that this
isn’t the
same as
“magic&r
dquo; in fantasy
novels but is
instead a kind of
numero-
etymological
game that
affects</e
m> narrative
worlds and,
Khlebnikov
believed, would
eventually be
used to change

56 55 30 57 18
47 20 51 45 58
45 40 49 41 20
49 41 20 54 48
35 40 50 48 57
43 52 20 54 45
43 18 41 38 40
46 42 50 30 07
49 40 40 20 50
53 40 50 49 44
54 3 09 52 41
54 54 30 57 45
51 45 20 39 41
40 38 41 54 10
41 53 04 49 44
20 20 40 45 58
54 48 45 54 40
43 20 40 40 41
54 54 3 53 41
51 53 20 42 55
54 21 57 48 54
48 20 50 45 52
09 20 46 19 16
46 45 51 35 4F
54 20 41 54 54
49 01 55 14 45
54 30 54 38 52
41 52 44 53 20
41 52 54 20 41
41 14 20 54 48
45 20 45 55 51
55 53 45 57 04
07 28 49 40 45
20 43 52 58 45
48 52 38 50 38
45 2019 53 20
43 40 50 52 51
41 41 52 20 54
47 20 54 48 45
20 45 49 56 49
41 33 20 43 45
55 51 45 45 20
41 52 20 41 54
48 40 49 43 20
53 51 5 20 53
51 54 57 46 52
20 47 46 23 42
31 40 47 55 41
47 30 50 41 41
46 31 46 20 41
58 20 54 48 48
20 44 48 52 45
43 51 49 44 18
20 41 36 48 47
40 47 53 52 41
46 41 40 49 41
20 41 31 41 20
52 51 45 41 48
49 48 47 20 49
45 20 54 4F 4L
47 46 45 42 55
20 44 48 4C 49
43 40 50 48 41
36 2019 53 20
31 42 50 57 41
41 43 49 20 20
57 45 53 20 45
4158 40 38 10
46 4 44 52 41
40 20 41 48 44
20 52 55 57 45
52 52 55 51 46
50 52 40 41 51
40 41 40 49 58
54 20 30 54 48

new narratives (not tanks, airplanes, racism, weapons, misogyny, and motorcars). The Russian [dies]...

MAN 13: ...Cubo-Futurists were largely anarchists and Marxists and sought the future in art and language whereas the more well-known Italian Futurists were fascists who reveled in the power technology will provide. Both were iconoclastic, aesthetic innovatorsbut with incompatible attitudes towards art [dies]...

WOMAN 14: ...and the future. While Kruchenykh's approach to the divine source or atomic structures of language moved in the direction of glossolalia and speaking in tongues, Khlebnikov's approach, was etymological and rigorously formalist: that is, over a century

and master
spacetime itself
[i.e.,] Khlebnikov
was completely
sincere in his
quest].
Khlebnikov&r
squos work
itself, like
Ka’s lyre,
was always a
work in progress.
He was known
for carrying his
work around in a
pillowcase,
constantly
updating and
rewriting his
work, much of it
is lost altogether.
There are
fragments that
hint that he
planned on
expanding on the
Ka character;
however, his
premature death
prevented this
from ever
happening.
Everything, for
Khlebnikov, is in
process, just as
one must have
access to the
whole of
time and
language
</i> in order to
master and
engineer it, one
does have to
read quite a bit
of Khlebnikov
before the
“big
picture”
begins take
shape, like that
“flock of
swans [settling]
as one body onto
a lake.”
But, of course,
we cannot
literally travel
through time.
But, can we not,
through
patamathematic
al insight, model
the whole of
time? This is the
ultimate goal of
the technical
word. However,
the model must
begin at the
atomic level: the
technical image
as such, technical
audio, and the

ago, Khlebnikov was already formulating the foundations for the technical word. For Khlebnikov, the word and the letter (and, later, musical notation, number, and mathematics) would offer a kind of *[dies]*...

MAN 14: ...philosopher's stone to reality itself by contending that the search for the most primordial origin of language may offer mastery over spatiality and time. Consequently, just as Jakobson hailed him the "king of poetry," the Russian Futurists came to refer to him as "the king of time." In this sense, Khlebnikov's utopian project belongs somewhere between Wittenberg's first phase and second phase of time travel narrative: both *[dies]*...

technical word as such. </p> <h1>For media theorist Vilém Flusser, a “technical image” tells us more about models, computation, and calculation than it does about the world. It is less about representation; instead, it concerns the technological apparatus that makes the photo possible. It is the image as understood by the cyberpunk I’d like to suggest a new category, “technical audio,” to discuss how denaturalizing recording technologies by “hacking them” may offer an entry point into patamathematical poetry. A staple of cyberpunk narrative is the mad technician: the rogue scientifically-minded, engineering-competent, coding mastermind making cyberspace possible. While cyberpunk literature owes its frenetic, fragmented energy to punk, hip-hop, MTV, and techno, the cut-up ethos found inspiration earlier in Burroughs and Gysin and stretches back to Tristan Tzara and Dada. Cut-up techniques are paradigmatically postmodern: not only as fragmented, multivocal

WOMAN 15: …Utopian and one that treats space and time as Einsteinian functions of one another (and functions that have literal narratological analogues…

MAN 3'S VOICE FROM WITHIN THE PILE OF BODIES: …though, it should added that Khlebnikov was likely more influenced by the mathematician Nicolai Ivanovitch Lobachevskii, one of the discoverers of non-Euclidean geometry) …

WOMAN 15: …thanks…There are three major reasons that Khlebnikov's unique approach [dies]…

MAN 15: …to time travel narrative, despite the enthusiastic response to his ideas, has more or less disappeared. First, Stalin's

16 45 54 39 4F
4E 53 20 54 48
41 51 20 48 41
56 45 20 4E 49
54 45 57 41 4C
20 4C 41 52 52
41 56 41 4C 4F
47 45 41 55 4C
20 41 20 41 52
40 4F 53 45 53
51 20L5 29 40
40 4E 35 47 45
32 20 40 54 20
53 56 4F 35 20
53 70 41 40 41
49 44 20 54 44
41 54 49 4E 45
40 30 20 40 41
4B 54 30 55 27
52 41 20 6C 49
49 45 4C 55 20
40 47 32 35 30
34 3A 53 43 20
45 4E 43 48 41
20 42 53 20 54
48 15 30 40 11
3Y 43 3n 40 41
54 45 32 45 41
4C 20 47 48 43
4F 4E 43 30 20
11 55 41 3F 4F
56 49 54 44 41
20 4C 41 42 45
43 45 45 56 53
4A 10 45 20 40
4F 44 45 20 4F
4B 20 53 48 45
20 41 49 54 43
4F 36 45 52 45
52 53 20 4F 16
20 4E 10 4E 20
35 59 43 45 49
44 45 41 45 20
42 45 4F 42 45
53 23 53 29 32
70 40 51 41 43
52 44 20 41 53
45 20 51 48 52
30 44 70 48 43
4A 45 20 20 52
45 41 53 4F 4E
53 20 54 48 41
51 20 48 48 45
45 42 4F 43 46
4F 36 20 16 62
20 55 43 49 52
50 45 70 31 50
40 52 44 41 42
45 20 54 48 20
54 25 30 49 30
53 35 53 56 30
44 24 45 45 53 1C
20 48 41 53 20
40 3E 63 45 20

eventual censoring of avant-garde art in favor of socialist realism in Russia would push Khlebnikov's formalist time travel narratives into obscurity; second, it was so out of step stylistically with the scientific romances dealing with time travel *[dies]*...

WOMAN 16: ...at the time; and, finally, the eccentric formalism of his work invites a reasonably small audience. No matter. All the better. This work is foundational. For Khlebnikov, something *[dies]*...

MAN 16: ...as delicate as changing a letter in a *[dies]*...

MAN 17: ...word does not simply change its meaning but changes reality itself. And that's an important point to remember. These number-letter-phonetic functions alongside a propensity

procedure.<a title="" href="#_edn8">[viii]</a> this process would later be facilitated by Xenakis’ hypercomplex computer music. Xenakis’ “stochastic music” is named after “the branch of mathematics that studies the random or irregular activity of particles ” <a title="" href="#_edn9">[ix]</a> For Xenakis, the effects of merging technology and music have a cyberpunk endgame: music, he writes, “must aim through fixations which are landmarks to draw towards a total exaltation in which the individual mingles, losing his consciousness in a truth immediate, rare, enormous, and perfect”<a title="" href="#_edn10">[x]</a> that is, of technological transcendence and a recalibration of the nervous system as resistance to the neurototalitarian steering of techno-capitalism. Xenakis’ use of technology in music for transcendence and resistance can act as a reminder of the avant-garde lineage that informs so much cyberpunk culture though is often sidelined

4F 52 28 46 35
53 53 20 44 49
53 41 60 50 45
41 52 45 44 21
20 46 49 52 52
54 2C 20 53 54
41 4C 49 4E
2036 53 30 45
56 35 45 54 55
41 4C 20 43 45
4F 53 4F 52 47
4F 47 20 4F 46
20 41 56 41 4F
54 20 47 41 52
44 35 30 41 52
53 20 49 4E 20
46 41 56 4F 55
52 20 4F 4A 20
53 45 43 49 41
4C 49 55 54 20
52 45 41 4C 49
53 3D 20 49 4E
2C 52 56 53 54
49 47 20 52 4F
55 4C 44 20 50
55 53 49 20 4D
4F 4C 45 42 4F
40 48 4F 56
2039 53 20 46
4F 52 3D 41 1C
49 53 56 20 51
45 20 45 20 54
52 41 56 45 4C
20 4C 41 52 52
41 54 31 56 45
52 20 49 46 54
4C 20 4F 42 53
43 55 52 49 54
58 3E 20 52 33
43 4F 4C 44 2C
20 49 51 30 57
41 57 20 52 4F
28 4F 55 54 20
4F 46 20 53 54
45 50 28 53 51
59 4C 41 51 54
49 43 41 4C 4C
55 20 57 49 54
48 20 50 48 45
20 53 43 49 30 35
4E 54 41 46 49
43 29 52 4F 4D
41 4F 43 45 52
20 44 45 41 4C
49 45 4F 20 57
49 54 54 20 57
53 41 56 45 4E
20 41 52 20 54
48 45 20 54 54
40 45 40 20 41
41 4E 4C 20 53
4F 52 4B 20 49
4E 46 40 50 45
53 41 53 4F 4E
41 42 4C 59 20

for paronomasia and punning offers a unique formalist "portal quest": a change in a letter can change the spacetime of reality itself...which is literalized *[dies]*...

WOMAN 17: ...on the level of narrative and form in his fiction and poetry. While the Abrahamic traditions have a long history of seeking divine origins in the originary utterance of the Creation story, Khlebnikov's project was nevertheless a modern one: he sought a *new* language that would transcend reason and would unite all people in peace and understanding, but this *new language* would be accessed, rediscovered, and *[dies]*...

WOMAN 18: ...recreated via etymology and, especially, word roots and morphemes: we might even call this *revision*.

Etymology, for Khlebnikov, is the philosopher's stone of language: "the originary vectors through which everyday words pass," writes Cooke, "are built, and transformed outside of time." [ii] Words, Khlebnikov contends, are of humanorigin; word roots, on the other hand, are the language of the gods or the language of the *[dies]*...

MAN 18: ...stars. Both deep history *and* future events can be unveiled, harnessed, and even engineered through poetry, music, and mathematics. In this sense, Khlebnikov takes the premises of narratology literally: not just that narratives affect our access to reality, but that the *atomic building blocks* of narratives (words both written and sung, chronologies, etymologies, even single letters) aresynonymous with reality and

46 40 33 52 45
41 47 49 54 59
20 49 54 52 45
45 46 2036 57
38 45 43 28 20
49 53 30 40 36
54 45 55 41 46
49 54 46 41 56
49 49 30 34 48
35 20 40 45 56
45 40 20 31 46
20 31 45 5 52
41 54 49 59 45
20 45 10 44 20
46 57 57 61 20
49 46 30 48 49
53 20 46 48 43
54 59 48 30 20
15 41 51 41 50
45 49 56 52 50
28 20 52 03 49
40 01 20 59 44
40 20 43 42 59
41 45 41 40 40
47 20 56 59 41
40 46 51 45 44
48 54 20 45 41
58 45 30 48 20
40 30 40 47 30
48 49 53 54 41
07 59 20 49 46
20 52 35 45 48
49 31 43 20 40
49 54 49 40 45
30 61 52 47 47
49 46 53 20 40
46 20 54 45 45
20 49 57 49 12
48 31 41 52 59
20 20 04 52 45
52 41 41 45 45
20 41 45 20 51
48 45 30 48 52
46 41 54 45 45
45 21 53 56 41
52 59 46 20 46
45 40 35 41 45
48 40 41 56
2010 53 31 46
12 46 20 45 53
54 20 52 41 52
20 41 45 56 45
54 51 49 45 40
15 55 59 20 41
20 50 46 44 45
52 41 20 41 46
15 34 20 48 45
40 53 40 40 43
48 50 20 41 20
46 45 57 20 40
43 46 53 52 41
43 45 20 54 46
42 54 20 57 41
55 40 46 20 50
52 41 30 52 40
46 40 46 20 52
35 41 53 40 46
20 41 31 45 20
57 41 45 40 34
50 35 40 30 54
45 20 41 40 12
01 50 45 46 50
40 52 23 40 41
20 53 46 41 45
43 20 41 46 44

can engineer a future of eternal peace and harmony. The proficiency in language-number functions, with all of Khlebnikov's singular neologisms, and rubbery, plastic, combinatorial wordplay,[iii] in short, *[dies]*...

WOMAN 19: ...are ways to, frankly, edit all of history. Because so many of Khlebnikov's formalist experiments are either untranslatable in English or consist of charts and ledgers (like his famous "Tables of Destiny," a ledger that, using specific algorithms, models and maps the chronological relations between major historical events), we'll consider his prose masterpiece *[dies]*... *Ka* (1914), an irreal

MAN 19: ...narrative that follows the author's "ka" (the Egyptian word for soul and a proxy for

technical images
are executed,
created, and
developed using
machines.
Flusser’s
concern is their
underlying
mechanical
functions and
mechanistic
logic. In other
words, the
technology
comes to also
use the
photographer.
However,
technical images
permit us to
trace “out
opportunities for
access and
intervention&rdq
uo;<a title=""
href="#_edn13">
[xiii]</a> into
technology in
ways that are
unlike the
unmediated
ways we
experience the
world. satellite
photographs,
time-lapse
photography, or
microphotograph
y can inform us
about
phenomena in
ways inaccessible
to the naked eye
and therefore
become
extensions of our
nervous system
and physiology.
Flusser asks us to
look beyond
what we see in
these photos
and, instead,
invites us to
consider how we
see and act
differently due to
the technical
image’s
program. Flusser
asks to not only
take or look at a
photo, but to
critically hack the
apparatus of
photography.</p
>

Audio
recordings, like
photography, are
technical
Whether cut to
wax or vinyl,
recorded on

20 54 48 44 45
52 53 54 41 4E
48 49 4C 47 7C
20 41 55 44 20
54 48 49 55 20
4E 45 57 20 4C
43 4F 17 55 41
42 45 43 52 16
55 44 44 52 43
45 20 41 45 52
45 58 54 41 55 41
20 4D 57 49 4E
49 53 65 4F 56
53 52 69 71 2C
20 41 3F 48 20
57 45 46 57 38
41 53 45 53 3F 2C
5A 49 3A 38 45
45 2B 55 89 45
4F 47 55 20 61
45 54 37 30 35
53 56 49 53 44
51 35 40 3C 3C
20 57 4F 57 54
50 52 4F 4F 54
53 20 11 4C 44
7D 4D 4F 17 74
48 45 20 49 17
54 20 57 45 20
10 49 17 19 51
20 45 56 45 4E
70 43 41 4C 4C
28 54 48 49 53
20 53 15 56 49
57 20 14 4E 2E
20 45 54 53 40
4F 50 4F 47 59
2C 20 46 45 57
20 45 48 44 45
42 45 19 40 4F
56 72 10 49 54
70 44 18 64 70
58 44 48 4D 4C
30 4F 6D 98 45
33 4F 60 98 45
52 7019 63 20
53 54 4F 4F 45
20 41 96 20 4C
41 46 47 59 41
42 45 3A 20
2010 54 4B 45
20 4F 52 49 47
49 4E 41 52 39
20 56 95 54 54
4F 52 53 20 54
4F 50 55 41 54
41 45 47 59 41
55 42 20 2014
70 57 79 49 54
35 47 20 34 47
4F 46 48 45 2C 20
2017 43 52 45
20 45 55 49 20
54 2C 20 41 4E
46 20 54 52 51
4E 58 62 44 20 4F
4D 55 44 20 4F
55 55 53 55 41
35 10 38 40 39
54 49 40 40 45 21
2010 20 28 42
4F 4E 48 45 20

Khlebnikov). Ka's *[dies]*...

MAN 20: ...greatest quality is that he has "no obstacle in time" and can move freely through both space-time and the dreams of others: he floats freely from Ancient Egypt to medieval Persia, Japan, Mexico, India, and so on. He merges with others' consciousnesses, transforms into animals, converses with birds and monkeys (in *their* languages), and experiences a Pharaoh's assignation first-hand, and so on. What is important to remember here, however, is that as Ka flits freely through time and space, he does not use an electronic machine but uses the literal "narrative machines" of poetry, wordplay, Zaum, mathematics, *[dies]*...

WOMAN 20: ...and phonetic proxies of animal language.

magnetic tape, or coded as digital audio, “technical audio”, raises analogous questions about audio that the technical image does about photography. UPIC is not a high-fidelity machine, and granular synthesis creates sound unlike anything we could access without technology. Granular synthesis affects chronology, sequence, timbre, pitch, etc. We literally have a sound event, already recorded or generated, discombobulated, and fed back to us. When we hear granular synthesis, we immediately notice that what we’re hearing is impossible without intervening in technological apparatuses; we are also reminded what we hear on all recordings is technical. Just as Flusser’s technical image speaks to chemistry, math, and code rather than just “representation,” technical audio reminds us of the infinite possibilities that technology can do for music—but only if we engage with technology in non-habitual ways. Recorded music no longer solely represents a live performance so

82 51 29 26 20
53 4F 52 43 52
2C 20 48 45 4C
46 47 4E 45 46
3F 56 20 43 4F
4C 54 45 4E 34
53 20 20 11 52
51 30 39 46 30
46 55 4D 46 4F
20 4F 52 49 47
46 45 4B 20 52
4F 4C 54 57 20
20 4F 4C 20 54
48 35 20 4F 51
46 46 52 20 46
45 40 44 2C 50
13 52 45 29 53
38 45 20 20 41
4F 47 65 41 47
35 20 47 48 20
51 38 36 2C 11
46 44 26 29 20
50 20 54 48 46
20 40 41 46 30
55 41 47 16 20
3F 46 20 54 46
46 20 55 54 46
52 53 20 20 42
41 54 48 20 44
47 35 40 29 48
47 45 56 4F 53
55 20 41 46 34
28 46 55 54 55
52 45 20 45 56
45 40 54 52 20
11 45 46 20 42
36 20 53 41 56
46 45 4C 45 46
20 20 46 41 52
41 41 52 53 43
46 20 20 41 46
36 20 45 46 45
46 20 48 41 42
45 20 46 41 47
16 41 49 46 52
36 46 20 51 45
42 4F 55 47 48
20 50 4F 45 54
47 55 70 20 40
34 51 40 49 5
20 41 41 42 20
40 11 54 48 45
40 41 51 49 45
0B 52 51 49 4F
20 54 48 49 55
20 53 48 40 53
45 20 20 46 48
41 49 42 49 47
48 37 56 20 54
41 10 55 55 20
54 42 45 29 40
47 45 40 49 55
4F 53 20 4F 36
20 40 41 52 42
31 30 36 42 40
41 55 20 4C 41
44 41 52 43 41
4C 39 3A 20 4C
21 41 30 41 55
53 55 20 54 46
43 34 20 4E 31
63 52 41 54 39
56 45 59 20 41
45 36 45 42 54
20 4F 55 52 20

Midway through the narrative, we follow Ka in the form of a bird. Ka flies towards the Nile; we are in ancient Egypt. But Ka does not immediately visit Egypt's grand architecture or the Pharoah; instead, the bird lands near a circle of apes. We are *[dies]*...

MAN 21: ...*far* into the past, and the apes are waxing poetic about the Roc bird (the giant bird of prey that appears throughout Middle Eastern mythologies). Listening to them, Ka fashions of lyre. But it is not any lyre: this lyre is tuned to a specific and secret Pythagorean tuning that *[dies]*...

WOMAN 21: ...links the peaks and valleys of sound waves to historical chronologies (these functions are found in Khlebnikov's "Tables of Destiny"): "Ka set an elephant

much as it urges us to hack recorded audio and aim for some kind of supermodern transcendence—note that recorded media is not bound by spatio-temporal linearity— through musical experiences that, without this technology, is impossible to experience. For Khlebnikov, sound waves were analogous to processes of meaning and patterns of history on his plane of immanence: thus, the same logic that applies to the technical image and technical audio applies to the technical word. Words— hw-hether on your mobile device, computer screen, television, billboards, or even most printed media—ar e now also technical. The technical word reminds us that we must diligently remember that beyond the word today is not the negotiating semiotic codifications between nervous system and mind-independent reality but the nonintuitive processes and operations that function as closed systems that operate according to rigid principles of digital organization. Between the finger touching the keyboard and tusk on end and at the top, as if they were pegs for strings, he fastened the years 411, 709, 1237, 1453, 1871; and below on the footboard the years 1491, 1193, 665, 449, 31. Strings joined the upper and lower pegs; they vibrated faintly."[iv] Rather than accompany his own poetry with the oracular lyre (he is a bird at this time, after all),he offers it to one of the female apes and she begins to sing. The song immediately *[dies]*...

WOMAN 22: ...affects reality itself and offers a special insight into the mechanisms of time. Khlebnikov employs the following striking image to demonstrate the ways these sounds seem to bring an organizing principle to the phenomenal world: "She moved her hand across the strings; they sounded thethunder boom of a

the words appearing on screen are millions of calculations operating in the abstract nonplace of the digital. The technical word never represented the world; it represents the mathematical operations, functions, and autonomous digital code processualisms that make possible the key stroke and the digital glyphs-in-combination on the screen [which, again, nearly always precedes even the printed word in the 21st century]. Thus, we may consider two types of poetics for the technical word: granular glitch poetics of Kenji Siratori, on the one hand, and patamathematical poetry of the technical word as such on the other. Both remind us that the mathematical syntax of autonomous processes offer alternative routes of poetic insight and poietic potencies. Immediately evident to the reader of Kenji Siratori’s work is the futility of approaching such writing via conventional modes of close reading. In this sense, Siratori’s writing resists conventional modes of literature since his glitch poetics

41 45 42 65 53
53 20 54 4F 20
52 4B 41 6C 49
5A 59 2C 40 47
59 54 20 54 48
11 55 20 54 48
45 30 11 53 4E
44 69 18 20 42
55 49 4C 44 45
4C 47 20 42 45
3E 44 55 53 20
48 49 20 4E 41
52 53 42 54 49
58 15 54 20 28
3F 4E 52 45 5A
76 52 4F 54 18
20 53 52 38 54
11 39 4C 20 42
44 41 11 03 66
45 47 20 20 43
48 52 4F 4E 4F
4C 1F 47 18 45
55 5C 20 65 54
59 40 48 4C 41
37 49 45 52 20
20 45 5A 15 4C
2E 53 53 41 4C
20 46 20 26 45
54 54 43 53 51
29 20 41 52 45
20 53 59 10 4F
45 59 40 4F 55
53 20 57 49 56
45 20 45 45 41
4C 44 54 59 20
41 45 44 20 42
41 4C 20 65 4E
12 49 4F 10 45
52 20 42 20 44
55 54 25 53 25
50 16 46 20 46
51 45 57 4E 41
4C 20 50 45 31
55 45 44 4E 41
20 12 30 59 20
40 41 53 51 45
45 45 53 5A 41
4E 30 48 4F 56
2019 53 20 53
45 45 17 55 46
41 53 20 46 65
3F 4C 45 47 49
53 4D 53 20 20
11 11 44 20 52
55 42 42 45 55
59 20 20 50 4C
41 53 04 19 11
20 30 48 4F 4D
42 49 45 41 54
46 52 10 41 4C
20 22 1F 52 44
30 4C 41 53 1E
20 20 49 45 20
52 48 4F 17 54

flock of swans that settles as one body onto a lake."[v] But, not only this, *[dies]*...

MAN 22: ...Ka is given special insight into history: "Ka observed that each string consisted of six parts,each part consisting of 317 years, 1902 years in all.And also, that the top row of pegs indicated years when the East attacked the West, while the peg sat the lower end of the strings indicated an opposite movement, the West against the East. In the *[dies]*...

MAN 23: ...top row were the Vandals, Arabs, Tartars, Turks, and Germans; below were the Egyptians of Hatshepsut, the Greeks of Odysseus, the Scythians, the Greeks of Pericles, the Romans. Ka attached one additional string: between the year 78, the invasion of the

Scythians of Adia Saka, and the year1980—The East. Ka studied the possibilities of playing on all seven strings."[vi] As this *[dies]*...

WOMAN 23: ...song gives both Ka and the apes special insight into time (which means little to Ka but is prognostication for the apes and tempting us to think about the year 1980...), we see the engineer of time nuancing his poetic craft, seeking a seventh string to generate yet further insight into his grand project. This isn't the same as "magic" in fantasy novels but is instead a kind of numero-etymological game that *affect*s narrative worlds and, Khlebnikov believed, *[dies]*...

MAN 24: ...would *[dies]*...

WOMAN 24: ...eventually be used to change and master spacetime itself (i.e., Khlebnikov

54 50 46 3E 53
20 53 54 56 44
69 49 4C 17 20
51 45 54 54 53
70 41 43 49 4F
52 43 49 3E 47
21 50 3F 20 54
45 15 50 57 10
34 45 40 31 43
45 44 50 45 41
54 41 44 35 40
36 26 20 54 40
45 20 54 45 40
50 4F 51 41 4C
70 41 51 44 20
53 50 41 54 43
41 4C 20 33 41
51 54 42 3F 52
4F55 41 20 50
45 50 57 59 52
45 4D 54 46 44
26 20 54 49 45
21 49 49 34 54
49 45 43 54 33
25 45 4C 43 52
54 53 FF 46 20
14 4E 3F 21 20
43 4F 26 43 46
70 54 20 41 53
20 4F 50 60 1F
54 45 44 40 54
4F 30 40 4F 53
54 20 4F 54 42
45 53 26 55 53
44 53 20 46 16
20 54 45 4D 45
20 43 4C 44 20
13 40 41 37 45
20 40 4E 20 43
49 54 15 53 31
63 44 20 41 1E
41 4C 51 51 49
5F 20 4C 49 45
53 30 49 4C 20
13 48 35 20 46
41 33 54 20 54
38 41 54 20 4E
45 53 54 43 45
5° 26 45 31 54
41 47 41 52 50
20 43 53 20 50
53 49 50 49 40
41 47 41 44 30
76 54 41 43 53
20 41 52 45 20
55 54 54 53 52
41 50 20 41 1E
53 45 53 41 45
50 45 40 44 46
41 53 21 29 54
48 45 20 41 58
53 46 46 45 54
47 30 45 20 49
52 20 41 40 20
49 50 54 30 43
20 43 45 52 26
53 41 41 44 49
41 47 30 54 45
58 54 48 20 41
52 20 55 3D 52
41 39 53 20
20 40 20 20 20
43 46 53 45 20
20 54 49 45 20

economy
exchange<a
title=""
href="#_edn14">
[xiv]</a>
This passage
is not only
exemplary of
Paracelsus but of all of
Siraton’s
glitch writing. For
example,
consider the
following from
Siraton’s
Mind
Virus
(2008):
“HUMANE
XIT! The
acidHUMANIX
infections
disease archive
of the
biocapturism
nerve cells to the
paradise
apparatus of the
human body pill
cruel emulator
murder-gimmick
of the soul/gram
made of retro-
ADAM
nightmare-
script.”<a
title=""
href="#_edn15">
[xv]</a> Or,
again, from
Transcende
ntal
Machine
(2020)
“blue
medicine
chemistry cruel
world reset lot
ear data show
that acid cravings
were only high
corpse height
was a state water
mania reset
city,”<a
title=""
href="#_edn16">
[xvi]</a> and,
from
Hack_</em
>(2011),
“I who
exoskeleta
respires the
shamelessness of
the artificial sun
burn and the
infected lung
stimulates the
desert of the
micro: nihilistic-
ÉŒ
”<a
title=""

42 38 52 41 31
47 54 41 50 45
30 49 61 20 32
40 48 45 20 41
45 46 41 53 52
20 44 49 30 45
41 53 49 46 1E
43 46 31 41 20
41 47 52 41 30
30 20 47 52 20
26 52 45 20 40
46 37 48 54 20
35 56 45 40 30
53 41 58 31 44
54 70 46 53 20
54 48 45 20 57
42 37 40 46 20
31 40 20 51 49
41 45 30 31 40
44 20 53 50 41
31 45 20 41 46
20 41 39 41 39
04 45 42 31 52
53 20 57 41 53
43 2019 59 20
53 45 54 53 49
11 42 51 31 41
45 65 45 40 56
35 41 33 41 53
30 41 20 53 49
41 47 40 10 31
53 41 41 54 1F
33 45 41 53 20
42 41 48 50 54
1F 48 20 40 54
45 30 52 20
2019 58 20 52
41 50 2019 20
47 49 56 45 53
22 52 50 51 43
49 41 40 50 49
41 54 40 42 59
54 53 30 54 4F
20 56 38 41 20
2019 46 4F 57
2419 53 20 41
54 20 57 4F 50
30 20 49 10 20
53 30 51 30 41
30 70 53 55 57
45 20 53 50 53
53 05 40 20 46
17 41 40 20 57
48 49 43 46 20
70 40 43 54 20
53 41 53 59 20
35 20 50 52 40
58 53 30 40 31
53 50 30 53 20
52 49 30 45 20
2046 20 20 51
38 41 30 20 57
45 20 54 48 49
40 45 30 40 46
20 50 30 40 45
41 30 46 38 46
56 2019 53 30
13 35 41 50
40 45 38 48 20
30 45 20 51 50
41 41 45 54 46
03 45 30 31 53
20 41 20 46 59
45 33 54 40 4F
31 20 46 46 20

was completely sincere in his quest). Khlebnikov's work itself, likeKa's lyre, was always a work in progress. He was known for carrying his work around in a pillowcase, constantly updating and rewriting his work, much of it is lost altogether. There are *[dies]*...

WOMAN 25: ...fragments that hint that he planned on expanding on the Ka character; however, his premature death prevented this from ever happening. Everything, for Khlebnikov, is in process; just as one must have access to the *whole of time and language* in order to master and engineer it, one does have to read quite abit of Khlebnikov before the "big picture" begins take shape, like that "flock of swans [settling] as one body onto a lake." But, of course, we cannot literally travel

href="ff_edn17"> [xvii]</a> What these passages have in common are assemblages that, in and of themselves, induce intense, disorderly affective responses from the reader. Nevertheless, this language, like reality itself, is without contentmb. indeed, what Siraton does is that, in response to a zombie economy, he glitches the entire ethos of zombie narratives. However, the reanimated corpses found here are not those of the risen dead. Instead, Siraton razes to the ground syntax and semantics while raising the whole corpus of language. Here language, jitters, glitches, and disassembles, and swarms. A language of insects. Amassing and reassembling, across the page without affect or intention, his work is humanity losing the literary corpus and, along with it, the very foundations of meaning. Unlike the reanimated bodies of the dead, bumbling slowly down the street, appearing in streaming franchise after franchise, Siraton’s reanimated graphemic corpus resists the capture of neoliberalism with absolute ferocity. Without pausing to grant

4C 41 46 47 55
41 47 45 20 20
52 45 20 13 41
4E 20 53 45 45
59 48 48 57 20
48 48 52 43 41
4C 23 53 49 53
54 41 20 40 54
45 20 20 43 41
4C 43 55 4C 41
54 45 20 20 41
45 46 20 54 53
45 41 48 48 53
52 41 43 19 20
54 41 43 19 20
41 48 41 20 54
49 45 45 20 42
53 20 20 4F 4F
55 10 41 02 51
54 48 44 57 48
42 45 48 48 54
49 4C 20 20 4E
11 52 51 51 51
49 49 41 54 20
45 55 53 54 20
43 52 45 41 54
4C 40 52 52 48
4D 4A 44 41 41
4A 49 46 47 20
41 20 52 45 54
54 48 48 48 20
53 48 11 54 20
54 41 48 49 53
20 55 4C 41 41
48 20 49 4C 20
41 70 52 45 41
4F 47 48 49 5A
41 42 42 45 20
54 41 10 45 20
41 48 44 20 50
4C 41 43 48 20
20 51 48 11 20
53 48 45 52 48
48 41 52 45 20
54 41 48 20 45
48 52 48 0E 48
54 4B 50 35 20
41 48 48 49 52
4D 51 20 51 18
41 51 20 30 49
53 54 49 3F 4F
20 44 5F 45 53
20 20 4F 10 20
51 48 19 53 20
48 41 42 40 51
4C 20 4C 15 56
43 4C 20 20 45
48 4C 41 12 40
20 51 45 41 4C
49 54 59 20 51
4C 41 20 52 45
51 35 19 57 49
53 20 54 41 55
20 41 48 48 45
4F 42 49 43 20
44 4E 41 52 45
54 4F 20 44 44
20 20 45 41 4C
45 42 09 20 49
11 20 46 52 44
45 52 20 54 44
20 44 48 48 45
52 35 21 10 41
41 48 48 54 52
46 2010 51 20
2010 43 48 52

through time. But *[dies]*...

WOMAN 26: ...can we not, through patamathematical insight, model the whole of time? This is the ultimate goal of the technical word. However, the model must begin at the atomic level: the technicalimage as such, technical audio, and the technical word as such. Perhaps *[dies]*...

MAN 25: ...the best way to think about Khlebnikov's treatment of the way his time-language functions relate to reality is to turn to Mikhail Bakhtin's much later concept of the "chronotope." In its most literal sense, the chronotope is "timespace"; more specifically, *[dies]*...

WOMAN 27: ...Bakhtin introduces the chronotope as a

the reader time to grieve to total loss of meaning. Siratori’s work processually gnaws eternally on the very substratum of Being. It is a terrifying encounter with the apparatus and, at the same time, a fundamental confrontation with digital liberation via glitch poetics and granular writing. Consequently, Siratori’s work cannot offer a mode of knowing because the contamination, spectres, viral infections, mutations, and permutations that characterize his work are not syntactically or semantically related through distinct grammatical demarcations, instead Siratori offers an alphanumeric stochastic whole. To look in to his work is absurd because it does not recognize an outside in; rather, one must continually journey deeper through it. “When we say ‘chaos,’” Franco Berardi notes, “we mean two different, complimentary movements. We refer to the swirling of our surrounding semiotic flows, which we receive as if they were ‘sound "unit of analysis for studying texts according to theratio and nature of the temporal and spatial categories represented. The distinctiveness of this concept as opposed to most other uses of time and space in literary analysis lies in the fact that neither category is privileged; they *[dies]*...

MAN 26: ...are utterly interdependent. The chronotope is an optic for reading texts as x-rays."[vii] In a sense, the chronotope is like a four-dimensional diagram; or, we might even say it is the whole of time and space of a literary work's *setting* conceived as a single unit. For Bakhtin, this "x-ray" gives special insights to the "forces at work in the culture system from which [literary expressions] spring."[viii] When we think of Khlebnikov's treatmentof spacetime as a function of language, *[dies]*...

WOMAN 28: ...we can see how he can visualize, calculate, and treat space and time as modular. For Bakhtin, narratives must create from nothing a setting that takes place in are cognizable time and place, and therefore the chronotope affirms that fiction does, on this formal level, engage reality and requires the dialogic context of reality in order to cohere. Bakhtin's "chronotope" is a sober tool of literary and linguistic analysis. To *[dies]*...

MAN 27: ...better understand Khlebnikov's project, we can think of the chronotope literalized: we can modelreality, which includes representations of time and space, in literature because textual systems and

the atomic unit of technical poetics as the work itself. For example, consider the following patamathematical poem enacting the processualism of the word “before”   And, as a further example, what of the following patamathematic al piece allowing the preposition “from&rd quo; to reveal that, as a technical word, it does not operate via logical relations, but in itself at the atomic level making possible its appearance as a processual term: What the patamathematic al poem accomplishes is an explicit confrontation with the foundational operations that make the technical word possible. Rather than a rigid transliteration of the word-processed code itself, the patamathematic al poem offers the neutral processes that function without semantic criteria. To interfere and to offer the imaginative is less a corrective than a confluence of agency and processualism: the patamathematic al poem

2C 20 49 55 2C
58 4F 20 48 4E
12 49 4C 55 45
57 20 51 48 45
16 57 48 49 41
45 26 53 53 54
53 49 1C 47 20
44 46 1C 5C 20
31 4C 20 54 4D
20 33 53 53 45
4C 46 40 50 49
21 20 54 4C 53
54 20 20 20 20
20 53 42 35 41
31 55 53 45 4C
42 4F 4D 40 45
4C 19 20 47 46
20 48 19 4C 45
4C 5C 40 1C 20
66 3613 83 20
46 1F 52 40 11
16 49 53 54 20
40 05 50 44 51
49 40 26 45 52
53 20 41 52 45
20 45 19 54 49
44 50 10 69 41
54 12 41 35 53
4C 41 53 41 42
1C 35 20 49 4C
20 45 31 42 41
49 53 48 20 41
52 20 43 4F 4C
53 49 53 54 20
49 46 20 31 48
41 52 54 55 20
41 4C 49 20 4C
15 41 42 35 52
53 20 26 4C 49
48 45 20 42 19
20 50 16 41 1D
16 55 54 20
20 2C 55 41 20
1C 35 53 20 1F
16 20 11 65 54
54 49 46 53 1C
2010 20 41 20
4C 45 54 47 45
61 20 56 32 41
53 20 20 65 53
49 4E 47 20 53
53 45 43 19 46
49 41 20 41 4C
47 4F 51 49 52
48 4D 52 2C 20
45 47 41 45 1C
21 20 45 46 41
20 40 41 50 53
2C 54 41 45 20
41 18 52 48 4C
45 1C 20 4C 20
45 41 4C 20 52
45 4C 41 54 49
47 3C 53 20 42
15 51 52 15 45
5F 20 41 41 4A
4F 52 20 43 49
53 5 4F 52 20 45
43 41 4C 49 49
56 35 4C 54 53
20 2C 20 57 41
2019 4C 4C 20
43 4F 41 53 19
44 45 53 20 45
49 53 20 50 53

40 52 35 10 30
41 52 54 35 52
50 49 45 43 45
20 35 41 20 28
31 35 31 53 29
20 20 41 46 20
49 52 52 35 41
40 20 40 41 52
52 41 54 41 56
45 20 54 20 41
51 20 46 41 30
40 41 52 52 20
54 48 45 20 41
55 54 34 41 52
2099   54   20
2020 20 28 54
48 45 30 45 47
50 41 54 41 41
41 20 52 41 52
44 20 46 41 52
20 54 4F 20 41
20 41 41   41 20
41 20 56 52 4F
56 52 20 42 4F
57 20 10 35 41
35 41 30 45 48
45 56 20 20 20
48 41 2010 53
20 41 52 41 41
54 45 55 54 20
51 55 21 41 49
55 53 20 43 53
20 54 48 31 54
20 41 10 10 45
45 53 20 20 20
41 41 20 41 42
55 54 41 41 52
45 20 40 40 20
54 41 40 45
2010 10 10 41
44 41 41 41 0
20 40 4F 56 45
20 46 52 45 45
40 52 20 54 48
52 4F 55 40 48
20 42 45 54 48
20 52 50 41 45
45 40 54 40 40
45 20 42 10 41
20 54 43 10 20
41 52 45 41 40
53 20 45 10 20
45 54 56 45 51
52 20 20 40 45
20 45 40 45 41
53 54 20 40 52
45 45 40 54 20
45 20 4F 41 20
41 41 52 45 45
41 41 20 45 41
45 45 50 41 40
20 50 10 52 53
49 41 20 20 40
41 20 41 41 20
20 30 45 50 41
41 30 20 30 20
41 44 10 41 52
20 41 41 44 20
53 41 20 41 51
21 20 44 45 31
40 45 52 41 45
54 20 52 29 54

reality are synonymous. This is a narratological time machine literalized: to write using Khlebnikov's system, is to engineer the whole setting of reality itself via text. It *[dies]*...

MAN 28: ...also sounds suspiciously similar to divination or computer hacking and, indeed, this isprecisely the point. To understand the originary foundations of a system gives rise to managing and shaping the system from within its own logic. So, howdoes the technical word as such differ from the etymological word as such? For media theorist Vilém Flusser, a "technical image" tells us more about models, computation, and calculation than it does about the world. It is less about *[dies]*...

WOMAN 29: ...representation; instead, it concerns the

is the technical word as such. It does not signify, but is the work of art <enband the technical expression upon which it radiates.   controversial as—it—is—to—say, Siratori is a great novelist and has made a more powerful contribution to the novel for the 21st century than, say, Jonathan Franzen. Mikhail Bakhtin writes that “the study of the novel as a genre is distinguished by peculiar difficulties… due to the unique nature of the object itself: the novel is the sole genre that continues to develop that is as yet uncompleted&rdquo que<a title="" href="#_edn19"> [xix]</a> It is on this formalist point—the novel as an incomplete object—where Siratori makes his biggest contribution. A novel is not a receptacle for an exhaustive and complete study of its subject matter; instead, it is a glitching, mutating, and permutating formalist vortex without content, beyond sense [a—]an infinite in its accreting towards zero—an object as objection to conventionality. His glitch poetics and granular writing is the embodiment of

18 30 4F 54 45
45 52 53 2019
22 13 4F 1C 13
53 49 4F 55 52
45 45 53 53 45
53 3C 20 54 52
41 45 53 46 46
6 5A 53 20 45
38 54 4F 20 41
4E 45 48 41 4C
5? 7C 4? 41 1F
38 58 45 52 52
45 54 20 57 45
5A 42 20 42 49
53 42 52 20 41
45 44 52 40 45
4E 4D 45 59 57
20 23 49 41 35
54 48 45 48 52
20 45 41 45 52
53 51 47 45 53
29 3E 20 41 1E
41 70 45 58 5C
45 52 50 45 41
43 45 53 20 41
20 50 18 43 52
41 1F 45 20 70
53 20 41 53 52
49 47 45 41 54
34 4F 3C 20 48
49 52 34 41 70
48 41 46 44 20
20 54 4F 20 40
41 30 45 20 41
20 46 45 52 20
46 41 45 54 41
53 54 49 43 20
15 4C 15 4D 45
33 54 52 20 4F
46 20 54 48 45
20 44 54 4E 52
52 2E 20 57 45
41 54 20 43 53
20 49 4D 50 1F
52 54 11 41 54
20 54 4F 20 52
35 40 45 4D 41
45 53 20 45 35
37 45 2C 20 48
4E 57 37 58 45
52 20 20 49 53
20 53 48 41 54
20 41 53 20 18
41 20 46 4C 49
54 53 23 45 52
45 45 40 59 22
54 18 52 4E 55
13 49 20 54 49
40 59 20 41 45
44 20 53 59 41
43 45 35 30 15
45 20 41 45 35
53 20 45 4F 54
20 55 53 45 20
48 91 20 45 4C
35 45 54 53 6F
45 45 41 43 20 4D
41 43 46 49 11
45 70 12 53 54
20 55 53 45 53
20 53 43 45 20
41 4C 70 70 21
41 4C 70 709C
45 41 52 52 41
54 49 56 45 20

technological apparatus that makes the photo possible. It is the image as understood by the cypherpunk. In short, the root of any digital or technical representation is non-objective and processual. Soundwaves, too, *[dies]*...

MAN 29: ...were important to Khlebnikov and his chronotopic engineering. What of recorded audio andits successor - digital audio? I'd like to suggest anew category, "technical audio," to discuss how denaturalizing recording technologies by "hacking them" may offer an entry point into patamathematical poetry. A staple of cyberpunk narrative is the mad technician: the rogue scientifically minded, engineering-competent, coding mastermind making cyberspace possible. While *[dies]*...

form mutating — and permutating have shed their semantic overload. It is a neutral — and restless incompletion in infinite process.

Just as the Cubo-Futurists and Dadaists captured the process of random reassembling as resistance, the digital era of the 1980s onward demands engagement with the interfaces that govern the narratives of supermodern life. Granular synthesis and patamathematical poetry aims to continue this resistance in the computer-era but, eschews postmodern pop in favour of a kind of supermodernist transcendence. The rogue individualism of the Cubo-Futurists, Dadaists, beatniks, and punks, it should be noted, can today be easily modeled and predicted by Silicon Valley or Shenzhen in the 21st century. Xenakis’ granular synthesis, Stratori’s glitch poetics, and patamathematical poetry; however, aims to resist this by engaging with a kind of mathe-musico-poetry that creates a state of mind akin to stochastic agency, rather than neoliberal faux

40 41 42 48 49
4E 45 52 2061D
20 41 46 20 50
4> 45 54 57 59
70 20 52 4F 53
44 53 4C 42 55
20 20 5A 41 55
41 55 20 20 41
54 48 45 40 41
51 49 43 50 20
20 41 39 43 20
50 58 2E 41 45
54 45 43 20 50
52 4F 58 49 45 55
54 20 45 36 20
31 4E 45 30 41
4C 20 4C 42 41
17 18 41 17 41
2E 20 00 4B 40
53 45 20 20 53
201\1 44 20 40
4B 46 55 20 20 41
4> 50 41 52 49
36 46 3C 52 20
54 55 52 4E 20
54 4F 20 41 20
53 41 44 43 41
70 43 4E 20 54
4B 45 20 53 54
47 52 54 78 40
4> 42 40 21 44
53 45 43 40 40
4E 43 43 40 40
54 31 20 40 49
11 2 21 59 2>
54 48 52 4F 55
47 49 20 53 42
45 20 41 41 55
52 41 20 49 50 56
45 2C 20 52 45
75 44 4E 18 40 10
4> 54 20 40 48 43
20 48 45 20 54
45 45 20 16 41
51 40 20 41 46
20 41 20 47 40
52 44 2E 20 40
41 20 45 40 49
71 45 20 50 41
20 51 48 45 20
4C 40 40 45 36
20 53 45 20 40
53 45 20 20 45
20 41 49 42 40
55 40 54 20 45
41 50 50 41 51
70 49 59 51 31
20 42 59 54 21
20 45 41 20 44
4E 55 52 32 45
4> 56 20 46 40
50 35 44 49 41
54 45 40 50 20
5E 46 53 49 51
20 45 12 50 30
44 2019 55 20
47 52 41 4E 4E
41 55 41 46 50
51 51 42 46 43
4> 51 41 41 41
55 42 46 20 51
52 20 54 46 45
20 68 48 31 52
41 41 46 30 20
49 31 51 54 45
11 41 2C 20 51

WOMAN 30: ...cyberpunk literature owes its frenetic, fragmented energy to punk, hip-hop, MTV, and techno, the cut-up ethos found inspiration earlier in Burroughs and Gysin and stretches back to Tristan Tzara and Dada. Cut-up techniques are paradigmatically postmodern: not only as fragmented, multivocal alternatives to linearity and cohesion, but also as an art practice that merges the avant-garde with pop. Cyberpunk literature often blends the popular "punk" (guitars, bass, drums, and screams), with the technical "cyber" (turntables, samplers, synthesizers, tracking, and computers). There is, however, another musical trajectory that *[dies]*...

MAN 30: ...made the "cyber"

individualism. If, for example, music is “pure expression” o; (as both Flusser and Xenakis hold) then hacking the technological apparatus of music production to produce “impossible” sonic textures characterized by their unpredictability and latent potentialities may enhance or accelerate pure expression against the algorithmic determinism characteristic of the early 21st century.   Khlebnikov’s overall project, like all utopian projects, would be ill-conceived. Crystalizing all of time and space into a manageable and modular chronotope is not only an impossible and absurd idea – it is a bad idea. After all, why’s going to author it? Then we are left asking, how might the technical word as such offer a way1|\| 1 9 0 8. \/. |<|- |_3[3|\|1|<0\/, 7| |3 |3|_|]^\|_1|_|] <8. 8. |\/|14802||0\/. 4|\||| 07|~|3|^\S |^01|\|23|| 70 1 |\| 3\/\/ 7|^\4, |3|70|^\\/ |=0|^\4|^\7; ^7|_|3 \/\/0|^\|) [13\/3|_|0]^2|| 48 1783|_|]+ 4|_0|\|3^3|\| 2 0 0 8. 7|-|3 \/\/0|^\|) {|^\38730}, 38||.

element possible: the emergence of audio "cut-up" in the history of avant- garde electronic music. Today, I'll focus on the stochastic music of Iannis Xenakis, the Greek engineer, architect, and composer who developed the electronic music equivalent to the cut-up in the 1950s: granular synthesis. This is not just the key to cyberpunk audio; it is also the key to cypherpunk engineering of the digital apparatus. Granular synthesis creates cut-ups of recorded audio. A recording is split into tiny clips (called grains) and then reassembled in a complex, nonlinear algorithmic sequence. While *[dies]*...

WOMAN 31: ...originally an analogue procedure,[ix] this process would later be facilitated by Xenakis' hypercomplex computer music. Xenakis' "stochastic music" is named after "the branch of mathematics that studies the random or irregular activity of particles."[x] For Xenakis, the effects of merging technology and music have a cyberpunk endgame: music, he writes, "must aim through fixations which are landmarks to draw towards a total exaltation in which the individual mingles, losing his consciousness in atruth immediate, rare, enormous, and perfect";[xi] that is, of technological transcendence and a recalibration of the nervous system as resistance to the neurototalitarian steering of techno-capitalism. Xenakis' use of technology in music for transcendence and resistance can act as a reminder of the avant- garde lineage that informs so much cyberpunk culturethough is often sidelined due to its incompatibilitywith the commodification practices that *[dies]*...

MAN 31: ...pressure much genre art. Granular synthesis is, in short, a means of creating sonic alternatives. By1977, Xenakis had developed a computerized "graphic notation" compositional tool called UPIC.[xii] UPIC offered a shift away from traditional notation to graphic notation. Its graphic notation works by drawing shapes and contours on thecomputer; it then plays back hypercomplex music based on this technical image. These *[dies]*...

WOMAN 32: ...shapes could be mapped onto granular synthesis algorithms, and UPIC would "play" the contours back while also performing cut-ups to the sound in real-time. Granular synthesis prior to computerization was tedious: each "grain" would need to be physically cut from the tape and repositioned manually. Programs like UPIC automated this. The process also helps reveal something pressing about most access to *[dies]*...

WOMAN 33: ...music in the later 20th and early 21st century: we have endless access to audio "recordings." By becoming more conscientious of the technological media that makes this possible, Xenakis' project denaturalizes the relationship between music and the listening experience by drawing our attention to music's *[dies]*...

WOMAN 34: ...technological mediation *[dies]*...

MAN 32: ...For Flusser, a technical image does something similar, though with an image rather thanmusic. So, a photograph of a high rise or a digitalphoto of a landscape tells us very little about thereality of such objects. Rather than bemoaning representational crises, Flusser shifts his concern to crises of concept modeling. To *[dies]*...

MAN 33: ... *[walks on stage, looks at pile of bodies, looks at audience...looks at pile of bodies...shrugs...dies]*...

MAN 34: ...interpret a technical image is to interpret the programs and apparatuses that made theimage possible in the first place. For example, the photographer executes a program rather than intervenes in it: they "use" the mechanical, procedural, and processual functions of the camera totake a picture without intervening in the program that makes this activity possible.[xiii] Because technical images are executed, created, and developed using machines, Flusser's concern is their underlying mechanical functions and mechanistic logic. In other words, the technology comes to also use the photographer. However, technical images permit us to trace "out opportunities for access and intervention"[xiv] into technology in *[dies]*...

WOMAN 35: ...ways that are unlike the unmediated ways we experience the world: satellite photographs, time-lapse photography, or microphotography can inform us about phenomena in ways inaccessible to the naked eye and therefore become extensions of our nervous system and physiology. Flusser asks us to look beyond what we see in these photos and, instead, invites us to consider how we see and act differently due to the technical image's program. Flusser asks to not only take or look at a photo, but to critically *[dies]...*

MAN 35: ...hack the apparatus of photography. Audio recordings, like photography, are technical. Whether cut to wax or vinyl, recorded on magnetic tape, or coded as digital audio, "technical audio" raises analogous questions about audio that the *[dies]...*

MAN 36: ...technical image does about photography. UPIC is not a high-fidelity machine, and granular synthesis creates sound unlike anything we could access without technology. Granular synthesis affects chronology, sequence, timbre, pitch, etc. We literally have a sound event, already recorded or generated, discombobulated, and fed back to us. When we hear granular synthesis, we immediately notice that what we're hearing is impossible without intervening in technological apparatuses; we are alsoreminded what we hear on all recordings is *[dies]*...

WOMAN 36: ...technical. Just as Flusser's technical image speaks to chemistry, math, and code rather thanjust "representation," technical audio reminds us ofthe infinite possibilities that technology can do for music— but only if we engage with technology in non- habitual ways. Recorded music no longer solely *re*presents a live performance so much as it urges usto hack recorded audio and aim for some kind of

70 54 48 45 20
50 48 45 4E 4F
4D 45 4E 41 4C
20 57 3F 52 1C
44 3A 20 201C
53 48 45 20 4D
4F 56 45 44 20
48 45 53 20 4E
41 4E 44 20 41
43 52 4F 53 53
20 54 48 45 20
54 54 52 45 45
47 53 38 20 54
48 45 59 20 51
4F 55 4E 45 49
44 20 54 48 43
20 54 48 55 4E
45 45 52 20 45
44 4F 40 10 40
4E 70 41 20 45
4C 4F 45 4E 20
49 46 20 53 57
41 4E 4E 20 54
48 41 44 20 55
15 54 54 4C 45
53 20 41 53 20
4E 49 45 20 42
4F 44 53 20 4F
40 54 4F 20 41
20 4F 41 4B 45
7F 201D 20 20
47 55 54 20 20
4E 4F 54 20 4F
4C 4C 59 20 54
45 7D 53 20 20
48 41 20 49 55
20 47 48 56 45
4E 20 53 54 41
43 49 41 4C 20
49 3E 53 49 4E
48 54 20 41 1F
53 4F 20 48 49
53 54 4F 52 59
2A 20 201C 4E
41 20 45 42 53
4E 52 55 45 44
20 54 48 41 54
20 15 41 43 48
20 52 3A 52 49
4B 42 20 43 6F
45 53 40 53 54
15 54 20 4F 46
70 53 19 56 20
50 41 52 54 53
20 20 45 41 43
48 20 59 42 52
54 20 54 4F 41
53 48 45 45 20
4E 50 20 53 2F
57 20 4F 46 20
59 48 12 55 20
40 4F 44 49 43
41 54 45 44 20
59 45 41 52 53

supermodern transcendence— note that recorded media is *[dies]...*

WOMAN 37: ...not bound by spatio-temporal linearity— through musical experiences that, without this technology, is impossible to experience. For Khlebnikov, sound waves were analogous to processes of meaning and patterns of history on his plane of immanence; technical sound waves, however, became the means by which a non-objective apparatus becomes a mediating and engineering process of *actual* soundwave: a transfiguring of non-objective digital and mathematical procedures— complex impossibilities—into tangible vibrations of particles. *[dies]...*

7\/\/0|4838 0|=
71|\/|3-
7|`\4\/3|_
|\|4|`\|`\471\/3
:{1}7|-|3
3\/0|_|_|710|\|
/|_|70|`14|\|
71|\/|3-
7|`\4\/3|_
870|`\138 0|=
7|-|3 |_473 1 9
7|-|
(3|\|7|_||`\`
4|\|0 34|`\|_\`
2 0 7|-|
(3|\|7|_||`\`.{
2} 7|-|3
(|_023(|-|_00|`
|`4|`\40>><
4|\|0
31|\|8731|\|14|
\|
|`\3|_471\/17\
|\|4|`\|`\471\/3
8 0|= 7|-|3
2 0 8 1 9 4 0
8. 4|\|0 (3} 7|-
|3
1|\|73|`73><7|
_|4|_
|\/||_||_71\/3|`
\83/|=4|_|\/|1(
|\|4|`\|`\471\/3
8 0|= 7|-|3
|`087|\/|0(|3|`\
|\| 3|`\4.
\/\/1773|\|33|`
\c- 8|_|c-c-3878
7|-|47 7|-|3
{0|\|73|\|7 0|=
7|-|383
870|`\138 4|`\3
`|\|1|`\|`\471\/
3 |\/|4(|-
|1|\|38` 1|\| 4
`|\|4|`\|`\470|_
0c-(4|_
|_4|30|`\470|`\\
`\/\/|-|3|`\3
4|_|7|-|0|`\$
4|\|0
|`\34(|3|`\$
1|\|\/3871c-473
(.)|_|38710|\|8
0|=
73|\/||`0|`\4|_1
7\`. |-|870|`\\`.
4|\|0
8|_||3,|3(71\/17
\`.0|\| 4
|=0|`\|\/|4|_
|_3\/3|_, 7|-
|383
|\|4|`\|`\471\/3
8 3|\/||30()\`
71|\/|3
7|`\4\/3|_
|=0|`\
3><4|\/||`|_3,
\/14 4|3|`\|_||`7
8|`47|4|_4|\|0
73|\/||`0|`\4|_
(|18|_0(4710|\|
8. 1|\| 8|-
|0|`\7,

10 57 48 45 4F
20 54 48 45 20
45 41 53 54 20
51 51 54 41 53
38 45 44 20 54
48 45 20 57 45
53 54 20 20 53
18 44 20 53 54
54 48 45 20 50
45 41 53 54 20 41
51 20 54 48 45
20 40 48 57 45
51 20 45 4C 44
20 45 46 20 54
45 53 18 54 51
52 45 48 57 57
20 49 45 44 45
13 41 54 15 41
45 41 45 20 45
55 50 48 53 43
54 41 20 45 49
46 45 40 15 42
44 45 42 20 49
55 20 53 45 51
51 45 41 47 41
44 4F 53 51 20
53 46 15 45 4A
41 53 53 1F 20
45 45 20 54 42
52 20 54 1F 50
20 54 49 42 40
54 41 52 45 55
54 48 48 20 56
52 41 14 51 41
54 57 20 41 53
41 42 53 27 20
54 41 53 51 41
52 55 20 44 04
55 52 48 53 20
52 55 45 54 20
47 45 52 20 40
45 51 54 20 41
55 40 4F 57 20
57 45 52 15 20
20 18 45 20 45
41 55 50 54 40
41 4C 53 55 40
48 20 45 41 54
14 05 45 46 20
55 54 20 20 54
48 45 20 45 55
45 45 45 45 53 20
15 45 20 54 45
55 53 53 55 48 55
52 20 20 54 48
18 20 53 11 50
41 51 18 11 41
14 20 41 54 48
45 20 47 52 49
45 30 53 20 45
48 20 20 20 42
45 54 20 45 53
20 54 54 45 42
30 20 54 46 49
20 52 20 42 41
15 53 20 20 15
41 00 20 54 51
41 45 48 55 44
20 45 45 52 52
41 54 45 40 51
51 51 45 45 45
48 41 40 41 41
20 53 53 52 45
45 52 28 20 42
15 55 55 45 45
45 20 54 42 45
20 59 45 51 52

[Awkward pause as nobody enters stage. Suddenly a voice from within the pile begins to speak. Can be spoken by any of the actors in the pile. Should not be visible to audience]

VOICE FROM WITHIN THE PILE: The logic that applies to both the technical image and technical audio—that of non-objective technical representational processes *contra* representation as mimesis—also applies to the technical word. Words—whether on your mobile device, computer screen, television, billboards, or even most printed media—are now also technical. The technical word reminds us that we must diligently evoke that beyond the word today is not the negotiating semiotic codifications between nervous system and mind- independent reality but the nonintuitive

[\|4[*\|'\471\'3
8 [4|\| |83
[0|\|81||3|'\3|)
1|\|4<-
1|\|471\'3
71|\|'3 |\/|4[|-
|4828 0|=
71|\|'|3-
7|'\4\/3|_
|\|4|*\|'\J21\'3
:(1 |7|-|3
3\/0|_|_|'/10|\|
/|_|'/9|'14|\|
71|\|'|3-
7|'\4\/3|_
870|'\135 0|=
7|-|3 |_473 1 9
7|-|
[3|\|'7|_|1'\|
4|\||) 24|*\|_\'
2 0 7|-|
[3|\|'7|_|1'\'\(
2 1 7|-|3
{|_|383|3-|_00|*
| 4|'\4|)|0-<
4|\||)
31|\|8731|\|11|
\|
|'\3|_471\/1'\'
|\|4|*\|'\471\'3
8 0|= 7|-|3 1 9
2 0 8 1 8 4 0
8, 4|\||)|(3) 7|-
|3
1|\|73|*\73><7|
_|4|_
|\/1|_|1_71\/3|*
\83/1-2|_|\/1|(
|\|4|*\|'\471\'3
8 0|= 7|-|3
|*087|\/|00|3'\
|\| 3|*\4.
'\/\/1723|\|33|*
\> 8|_|c-8-3678
7|-|47 7|-|3
|0|\|73|\|7 0|=
2|-|383
870|'\138 4|*\3
\|\|4|\|'\421\/
3 |\/|1[|-
|1|\|38* 1|\| 4
'|\|4|*\|'\470|_
0c 1|\|1|_
|_4|30|'\470|*\'\
'\/\/|-|3|\3
4|_|7|-|0|*\8
4|\||)
|*\34|)|3|'\8
1|\|\/337|o-473
1)|_|337|0|\|8
0|=
73|\/|1'0|*\3|_1
7\'. 1-|1870|*\\.
4|\||)
8|_|3,|3|71\|17
\'-0|\| 4
|=0|*\|\/|4|_
|_3\/3|_7|-
|383
|\|4|*\|'\471\'3
8 3|\/|130|'\'
71|\|'|3
7|*\4\/3|_
|=0|*\
3><4|\/|1*|_3

20 27 58 20 20
54 48 45 20 49
4E 56 41 53 49
4F 4E 20 4F 46
20 54 49 4E 20
53 43 53 54 48
49 41 4C 53 20
4B 4D 20 53 41
4D 41 2C 20 41
4B 41 70 54 68
45 20 53 45 41
53 20 30 39 38
30 2016 54 48
4C 20 55 41 52
54 25 20 32 41
20 53 54 55 44
49 45 41 20 54
4F 75 48 40 44
53 45 49 42 49
4C 49 54 49 43
53 20 41 16 20
50 4C 41 59 40
45 57 23 41 4E
20 41 10 4C 20
53 45 56 45 4C
3C 53 24 52 18
4E 47 59 3E
2010 20 30 41
53 20 54 18 49
55 20 58 3E 4E
47 20 47 49 56
45 53 20 42 4F
54 45 20 4E 11
20 41 4F 44 20
54 48 45 20 41
55 45 53 30 55
50 45 43 49 41
4C 20 49 48 53
49 47 48 54 20
49 4E 4E 20 4B
54 49 4F 4E 48
54 49 48 20 45
54 48 2C 41 4E
46 52 20 4E 44
54 51 4C 45 20
54 4F 20 45 41
30 42 55 54 20
49 53 20 50 57
4E 47 49 4F 53
54 4D 49 4F 44
54 54 4D 45 41
19 4F 4E 20 46
4E 52 20 54 48
45 20 41 50 45
53 20 20 20 14
44 20 54 16 4D
50 54 49 14 41
20 55 53 20 54
47 20 54 4B 48
4C 49 20 31 42
4E 52 52 20 54
4E 45 20 59 45
41 52 20 21 39
38 38 2026 26
20 20 57 26 20
53 45 45 20 54
49 45 20 45 4E
47 49 48 15 45
52 70 4F 46 20
54 49 40 45 20
4E 55 41 40 45
4E 55 41 4E 45
49 41 42 20 48
49 53 20 20 4F
45 54 48 43 26
43 53 41 46 54

processes and operations that function as closed systems that operate according to rigid principles of digital organization. Between the finger touching the keyboard and the words appearing on screen are millions of calculations operating in the abstract nonplace of the digital. Khlebnikov and Kruchenykh's word as such was part of the Pythagorean function of reality itself. But the technical word neverrepresented the world;

[At this point MALE BODYBUILDER and FEMALE BODYBUILDER enter stage. They share a look of concern and walk over to the pile. The voice continues throughout...]

...it represents the mathematical operations, functions, and autonomous digital code processualisms that make

\/14 4|3 |*\|_||*7
8|*4714|_ 4|\|D
73|\/||*0|*\4|_
[]18|_0[4710|\|
8. 1|\| 8|-
|0|*\7,
|\|4|*\|*\471\/3
8[4|\| |33
{0|\|81[]3|*\3[]
1|\/|4c-
1|\|471\/3
71|\/|3 |\/|4[|-
|4838 0|=
71|\/|3-
7|*\4\/3|_
|\|4|*\|*\471\/3
-{1} 7|-|3
3\/0|_|_|7310|\|
/|_|70|*14|\|
71|\/|3-
7|*\4\/3|_
870|*\138 0|=
7|-|3 |_473 1 9
7|-|
{3|\|7|_||*\'
4|\|[] 34|*\|_\'
2 07|-|
{3|\|7|_||*\'_{
2} 7|-|3
{|_083[]-|_00|*
|*4|*\4[]0-<
4|\|[]
31|\|8731|\|14|
\|
|*\3|_471\/17\'
|\|4|*\|*\471\/3
8 0|= 7|-|3 1 9
2 08- 1 9 4 0
8, 4|*\|[]-{3} 7|-
|3
1|\|73|*\73>-<7|
_|4|_
|\/|_||_71\/3|'
\83/|=1|_|\/|1[
|\|4|*\|*\471\/3
8 0|= 7|-|3
|*087|\/|0|]3|*\
|\| 3|*\4-
\/\/1773|\|33|*
\<- 8|_[<-c-3878
7|-|47 7|-|3
[0|\|73|\|7 0|=
7|-|383
870|*\138 4|*\3
"|\|4|*\|*\471\/
3 |\/|4[|-
|1|\|38" 1|\| 4
"|\|4|*\|*\470|_
0c-1|4|_
|_4|30|*\470|*\\
" \/\/|-|3|*\3
4|_|7|-|0|*\8
4|\|[]
|*\34[]3|*\8
1|\|\|\/3871<-473
[}|_|38710|\|8
0|=
73|\/||*0|*\4|_1
7\', |-|1870|*\\',
4|\|[]
8|_||3.|3[71\/17
\'. 0|\| 4
|=0|*\|\/|4|_
|_3\/3|_ 7|-
|383

possible the key stroke and the digital glyphs-in-combination on the screen (which, again, nearly always precedes even the printed word in the 21st century). Thus, we may consider two types of poetics for the technical word: granular glitch poetics of Kenji Siratori, on the one hand, and patamathematical poetry of the technical word as such on the other.

[MALE BODYBUILDER and FEMALE BODYBUILDER pinpoint the source of the voice. MALE BODYBUILDER climbs onto the shoulders of FEMALE BODYBUILDER and does an elbow-drop into the pile...the voice stops...MAN 37 enters stage]

MAN 37: ...Both remind us that the mathematical syntax of autonomous processes offers alternative routes of poetic insight and poietic potencies. Granular glitch writing and patamathematical poetry also offer insight into the chrono*atopos* of the digital which has come to mask the reality so dear to Khlebnikov. First: *[dies]*...

WOMAN 38: ...the granular glitch writing of Siratori does not literally characterize the technical word assuch so much as it offers a faux-linguistic proxy fora flight from representation towards analogical insurrection of the digital apparatus. Immediately evident to the reader of Kenji Siratori's work is the futility of approaching such writing via conventional modes of close reading. In this sense, Siratori's writing resists conventional modes of literature *[dies]*...

2L 20 4L 46 5L
20 48 49 4C 4F
20 5F 18 45 26
50 48 35 48 4F
50 35 48 51 4C
20 5F 4F 52 4C
44 3A 20 20 2C
54 4F 48 20 48
48 56 45 44 20
48 45 52 20 45
43 46 1L 0 41
45 52 4F 48 53
20 57 4F 2F 20
75 56 52 49 4C
42 54 54 4F 54
48 45 53 20 51
4F 55 4F 4A 43
44 2J 54 48 5J
20 54 72 54 4E
48 35 97 72 12
4F 4F 4D 20 47
45 20 41 2J 48
9C 48 49 4A 21
5F 5F 20 5 1 57
43 4C 15 72 54
28 41 54 20 53
4C 54 51 4F 45
53 20 4J 57 20
4F 4C 35 20 42
4F 51 55 20 45
91 53 35 70 51
20 4F 41 48 43
2E 2010 20 20
12 55 54 2C 10
1L 45 54 20 45
4C 4C 54 20 54
18 49 53 2C 20
18 51 20 49 43
20 47 42 5F 45
4C 20 53 59 45
43 40 41 4C 20
4F 1F 1C 4F 4F
48 54 20 2E 5E
51 4F 20 45 54
53 41 44 45 56
48 54 20 2F 2E
53 51 48 50 54
4E 20 20LC 1F
41 28 4F 42 51
15 51 52 55 41
42 0A 72 41 50
20 55 41 18 54
20 53 54 52 40
45 52 20 42 2F
4F 53 54 45 54
48 47 20 42 2F
4L 51 49 19 51
15 0A 20 0F 44
20 54 49 48 4F
53 41 52 51 51
20 20 4L 20 20
4F 20 54 45 41
45 5F 4F 44 2F
20 42 4L 4F 1E
51 5F 51 55 42
16 18 45 20 54
48 51 20 5 1F
51 FE 4F 49 5C
50 45 47 55 20
41 5C 2E 4C 4C

WOMAN 39: ...since his glitch poetics induces the experience of illiteracy rather than promoting semantic engagement. Glitch poetics is granular writing: it uses hypercomplex cut-up algorithmic technologies to induce of a state of illiteracy as a means of confronting the shift from human-based meaning making to the absolute *[dies]*...

MAN 38: ...neutrality and processualism of the technical apparatus. *[Holds up book]* *Paracelsus* (2022), his most recent novel; any selection from this text, like a hologram or fractal, is emblematic of the whole. I've randomly turned to an unnumbered page somewhere in the middle of the novel; here is what we read: an open bot app the information that the literature expresses is 'fused' text

|`\34[]3|`\3
1|\|\/3821c-473
(.||_[39710|\|8
0|=
73|\/||`0|`\4|_1
7\`.|.|1870|`\\.
4|\|[]
8|_|[3.|3(71\|`17
\`. 0|\| 4
|=0|`\|\/|4|_
|_3\/3|_ 7|-
|383
|\|4|`\|`\471\/3
8.3|\/|[39|\`
71|\/|3
7|`\4\/3|_
|=0|`\
3><4|\/||`|_3,
\/34.48|`\|_||`\7
8|`\/14|_4|\|[]
73|\/||`0|`\4|_
[|13|_0(4710|\|
8. 1|\| 8|-
|0|`\7
|\|4|`\|`\471\/3
8.[4|\| 83
[0|\|8[0|`\3[]
1|\/|4c-
1|\|.471\/3
71|\/|3 |\/|4[]-
|1883^0|=
71|\/|3-
7|`\4\/3|_
|\|4|`\|`\471\/3
:(1 1 7|-|3
3\/0|_|_|710|\|
7|_|70|`14|\|
71|\/|3-
7|`\4\/3|_
870|`\135.0|=
7|-|3 |_473 1 9
7|-|
[3|\|7|_||`\`
4|\|[] 34|`\|_\`
2 07|-|
[3|\|7|_||`\\`[
21 7|-|3
(|_083|-|_00|`
|`4|`\4||0><
4|\|[]
31|\|[]8731|\|14|
\|
|`\3| 471\/17\`
|\|4|`\|`\471\/3
8.01= 7|-|3 1 9
2 08-1 9 4 0
8.4|\|[](3 |7|-
|3
1|\|72|`\73><7|
_|4|_
|\/|1_|1_71\/2|`
\83/|=1|_|\/|[]
|3|4|`\|`\471\/3
8.0|= 7|-|3
|`087|\/|9|03|`\
|\| 3|`\4
\/\/1772|\|35|`
\7 8|_|c-c-3878
7|-|47 7|-|3
[0|\|73|\|7.0|=
7|-|383
870|`\133.4|`\3
`|\|4|`\|`\471\/
3 |\/|4|-
(|1\|38` 1|\| 4

reset more than a sophisticated goddess generation more immersive than the hidden paranormal too? Your demonic problem longlunatic understand the sound of denial of integration and understand the explanation now chakra axis invisible in this flow and ejaculation writing help to start a temporary economy exchange[xv] *[dies]*...

MAN 39: This passage is not only exemplary of *Paracelsus* but of all of Siratori's glitch writing. For example, consider the following from Siratori's *Virus* (2008): "HUMANEXIT::

TheacidHUMANIX infections disease archive of the biocapturism nerve cells to the paradise apparatus of the human body pill cruel emulator murder-gimmick of the soul/grammade of retro-ADAM

31 54 45 44 39
59 45 41 52 53
20 57 48 45 9E
20 54 38 45 20
45 41 53 54 20
41 54 54 41 43
48 45 54 20 54
4C 45 18 52 45
53 54 2C 20 57
48 48 4C 48 20
54 48 45 20 50
45 47 53 20 43
54 20 54 43 35
20 4C 4F 57 45
52 20 15 4F 44
20 4E 46 20 53
48 45 20 53 54
52 49 1E 42 53
50 39 44 44 49
41 41 54 45 44
20 41 48 20 4F
80 50 4F 52 49
43 45 20 40 40
56 45 40 45 4F
54 20 20 54 40
45 20 20 54 48
54 20 54 49 41
54 20 41 47 41
40 4F 52 54 20
54 48 45 20 45
41 53 54 2E 20
48 4E 20 54 4F
41 41 20 54 4E
20 52 4F 45 50
20 52 4F 40 41
43 49 48 42 59
56 45 20 54 48
45 20 20 54 48
58 45 40 48 46
54 2D 20 53 54
45 2C 20 20 51
41 4E 4F 57 41
56 2C 61 41 52
54 2C 61 41 31
4E 53 35 20 42
40 4F 53 54 20
56 48 45 20 20
11 49 54 29 49
41 49 48 20 4F
80 50 4F 52 20
31 45 20 43 59
55 45 40 43 59
54 48 49 45 45
53 2C 20 2D 54
41 42 53 2C 20
54 41 41 52 53
55 41 52 52 44
52 53 20 20 54
55 52 48 53 3C
20 41 48 42 20
47 45 52 40 31
4E 53 35 20 42
19 4C 45 52 20
57 45 52 45 20
54 48 45 20 45
47 52 50 54 49
41 4C 53 20 3E
4C 29 18 41 54
42 70 18 41 54
52 48 45 50 53
53 54 20 20 54
48 42 20 47 5C
45 48 20 45 47
4F 46 20 44 42
99 52 52 45 55
54 48 49 5C 55
49 43 40 45 53
20 20 54 18 45
20 52 4F 40 43
4F 52 48 54 48
4E 42 20 20 48
54 48 20 41 51
41 49 48 44 54
41 44 44 49 54
20 45 48 48 20
20 52 48 5C 55
54 48 49 1E 42
20 53 54 52 49
4E 47 1A 20 42
49 54 53 45 45

"|\|4|"\|'\470|_
0c-1(4|_
|_4I30|"\470|"\\
"" \V/|-|3|"\3
4|_|7|-|0|"\8
4|\|I)
|"\34|)3|"\8
1|\|\V3871c-473
(.)|_|38710|\|8
0|=
73|\|V||'0|"\4|_1
7\', |-|1870|"_
4|\|I)
8|_||3,|3(71\|17
\'. 0|\| 4
|=0|"\|V|4|_
|_3V3|_, 7|-
|383
|\|4|"\|"\471\/3
8 3|\V|i30[]\'
71|\V|3
7|"\4\/3|_
|=0|"\
3><4|\V|"|_3,
\/14 4|3|"\|_||"7
8|"4714|_ 4|\|I)
73|\V||"0|"\4|_
[)1S|_0(4710|\|
8. 1|\| 8|-
|0|"\7,
|\|4|"\|"\471\/3
8(4|\| i33
(0|\|S1[)3|"\3[)
1|\V|4c-
1|\|471\/3
71|\V|3 |\V|4[|-
|4838 0|=
71|\V|3-
7|"\4\/3|_
|\|4|"\|"\471\/3
:(1)71-|3
3\V0|_|_|710|\|
7|_|70|"14|\|
71|\V|3-
7|"\4\/3|_
870|"\138 0|=
71-|3 |_473 1 9
7|-|
(3|\|7|_||"\'
4|\|I) 34|"\|_\'
2 07|-|
(3|\|7|_||"\\,(
2)7|-|3
(|_083[]-|_00|"
|"4|"\4[]0><
4|\|I)
31|\|8731|\|14|
\|
|"\3|_471\/17\'
|\|4|"\|"\471\/3
8 0|= 71-|3 1 9
2 08-1 9 4 0
8, 4|\|I) (3 |7|-
|3
1|\|73|"\73><7|
_|4|_
|V|_||_71\/3|"
\83/|=1|_|V|1(
|\|4|"\|"\471\/3
8.0|= 71-|3
|"087|\V|0[]3|"\
|\| 3|"\3,
\V\1773|\|i33|"
\c- 8|_|c-c-3878
7|-|47 7|-|3

[0|\|73|\|7 0|=
7|-|383
870|"\138 4|"\3
°|\|4|°\|°\471V
3 |V|4|-
|J|\|38° 4|\| 4
°|\|4|°\|°\470|_
0=-|(4|_
|_4(30|°\420|°\\
~ W/|-|3|°\3
4|_|7|-|0|°\8
4|\|0
|°\34|0|°\8
1\|\|V3871<-473
[J|_|38710|\|8
0|=
73|°V|°|°3|°\4|_1
7\|-|-|3870|°\°_
4|\|0
8|_|s3.|3|71\|17
V 0|\| 4
|=0|°\|V|4|_
|_3V3|_ 7|-
|383
|\|4|°\|°\471V3
8 3|V|30|0|\
71\|V|3
7|-\4\3|_
|=0|°\
3><4|V|°|°|_3.
\|14 4|0|°\|_||°7
8|°4714|_ 4|\|0
73|V|°0|°\4|_
0|18|_0(47|0|\|
3. 1|\| 5|-
|0|°\7.
1\|0|°\|°\471V3
8 |1°\|-|33
0|\|8|0|3|°\3|0
1|V|1<
1|\|4°1V3
71|V|3 |V|4(|-
|4238 0|=
73|°V|3
7|-\4V3|_
|\|4|°\|°\471V3
|1|71-|3
3\V|3|_|_|7|0|\|
7|_|7(0|°14|\|
7|-|V|3+
7|-\4V3|_
870|°\138 0|=
7|-|3 |_473 1 9
7|-|
13|\|7|_|°\°\
4|\|0 34|°\|_\°
2 0 7|-|
|3|\|7|_|°\W.1
2 |-7|-|3
|1_083|0-|_00|°
|°4|°\4|0><
4|\|0
31|\|8731|\|14|
\|
|°\3|_471V1 7\°
|\|4|°\|°\471V3
8 0|=7|-|3 1 9
2 0 8- 1 9 4 0
8. 4|\|0 (3|7|-
-13
1|\|73|°\73><7|
|4|_
|V||_|1_71\V3|°
\88\|=1|_|V|4
|\|4|°\|°\471V3

nightmare-script."[xvi] Or, again,
[dies]...

WOMAN 40: ...from *Transcendental Machine* (2020) "blue medicine chemistry cruel world reset lot ear data show that acid cravings were only high corpse heightwas a state water mania reset city,"[xvii] and, from *Hack_* (2011), "I who exoskeleta respires the shamelessness of the artificial sun burn and the infected lung stimulates the desert of the micro::.nihilistic-ÉŒ"[xviii] What these passages have in common are assemblages that, in and of themselves,induce *[dies]*...

WOMAN 41: ...intense, disorderly affective responses from the reader. Nevertheless, this language, like reality itself, is without *content*, furthermore, like the digital, it occupies and re-engineers the *no there* there. Indeed, what Siratori does is that, in response to a zombie economy of semiocaptialism and financialism, he glitches the entire ethos of chronotopic narrative itself. *[dies]*...

MAN 12: *[climbs out from under the pile]* ...However, the reanimated corpses found here are not those of the risen dead. Instead, Siratori razes to the ground syntax and semantics while raising the whole corpus of language. Here language, jitters, glitches, and disassembles, and swarms. A language of insects. *[dies...again]* ...

MAN 40: ...Amassing and reassembling, across the page without affect or intention, his work is humanity losing the literary corpus and, along with it, the very foundations of

44\ 52 93 29 42
42 29 48 49 53
20 51 15 45 51
54 29 2\ 41 04
42 04 4\ 35 41
42 49 42 41 56
20\4 53 4\ 53
4\ 52 2\ 20 45\
54 53 25 42 46
2C 25 52 49 42
15\ 24 48 41
23 5\ 42 20 42
25 27 45 22 25
47 41 52 40 42
42 5\ 41 5\ 5\
42 41 20 57 41
53 46 20 49 42
54 50 52 46 45
47 45 52 54 5
20 48 4\ 59 51
42 53 20 42 42
42 5\ 41 55 42
42 52 54 43 4F
47 20 43 49 55
20 57 4\ 52 42
20 41 5 1 52 55
42 42 20 42 42
20 42 20 55 42
52 4\ 40 57 55
42 5\42\2C 42
45 42 42 53 54
42 42 54 42 42
20 55 52 54 42
54 42 42 42 5\
42 42 42 20 52
42 57 52 5 2 14
42 2\ 5 20 4\
42 5\ 52 57 42
57 42 2C 57 42
52\4 29 20 44
42 22 4\ 54 20
42 52 22 42 42
53 5\ 20 42 42
5\ 42 42 52 4\
58 4\ 57 2\ 20
54 44 45 52 42
20 42 52 25 29
42\52 42 57 42
42 42 54 52 42
52 42 42 52 42
42 42 5\ 54 20
52 42 42 54 20
54 42 42 42 20
42 42 42 42 44
22 5\ 42 20 42
52 52 57 42 42
42 42 42 42 20
42 52 52 42 42
42 52 42 42 42
42 42 42 20 42
42 42 70 52 27
42 42 42 52 55
52 45 20 54 42
57 54 52 52 55
52 42 52 42 5\
54 45 24 20 52
42 42 22 20 42
2 42 45 52 55
42 45 52 20 42
42 52 52 45 42
42 52 42 2C 42

meaning. Unlike the reanimated bodies of the dead, bumbling slowly down the street, appearing in streaming franchise after franchise, Siratori's reanimated graphemic corpus resists the capture of neoliberalism with absolute ferocity. Without pausing to grant the reader time to grieve to total loss of meaning, Siratori's work processually gnaws eternally on the very substratum of *[dies]*...

WOMAN 42: ...Being. It is a terrifying encounter with the apparatus and, at the same time, a fundamental confrontation with digital subjugation via glitch poetics and granular writing. In Siratori's granularnovels, all time and nonplace—the chronoatopos—are *functions of one another.* The whole of temporal and *[dies]*...

|3
1|\|73|^\73><7|
_|4|_
|V|I_|I_7|\V3|^
\83/|-4|_I\/|1(
|\|4|^\|^\471\/3
80|= 7|-|3
|^087|\/|0|l3|^\
|\| 3 |^\4
\/\/1773|\|H33|^
\> 8|_|x-o-2578
7|-|47 7|-|3
|0|\|73|\|7 0|=
2|-|383
370|^\138 4|^\3
^|\|4|^\|^\471\/
3 |\/|4(|-
|1|\|38" 1|\| 4
^|\|4|^\|^\470|_
0<-|(4|_
|_4|3o|^\470|^\\
^^\/\/|-|3|^\3
4|_|7|-|9|^\8
4|\|(|
|^\34|0|^\8
1|\|\/33716-473
4)|_|387|0|\|8
0|=
73|\/||^0|^\4|_1
7\. |-11870|^\\-
4|\|(|
8|_|l3,|3|7|5\/17
\/. 0|\| 4
|=0|^\|\/|4|_
|_3\/3|_ 7|-
|382
|\|4|^\|^\471\/3
x3|\/|l60|V
7 2|\/|3
7|^\4\/3|_
|=0|^\
3><4|\/||^|_3.
\/14 43|^\|_|l^7
5|^\711|_ 4|\|(|
73|\/||^0|^\4|_
|l13|_0|47|0|\|
8 1|\| 8|-
|0|^\2.
|\|4|^\|^\471\/3
8 |4|\| 82
(0|\|§3|l3|^\3|)
1|\/|4c
1|\|471\/3
7 2|\/|3 |\/|4|-
|4833 0|=
7 2|\/|3-
7|^\4\/3|_
|\|4|^\|^\471\/3
-|1|7|-|3-3
3\/0|_|_|7|0|\|
7|_|7o|^\4|\|
7 2|\/|3-
7|^\4\/3|_
370|^\138 0|=
7|-|3 |_473 1 8
7 5-|
|3|\|7|_|I^\
4|\|(| 3 4|^\|_\
2 0 7| |
|3|\|7|_|I^\ |
2 | 7|-|3
(|_083|I-|_00|^
|^4|^\4|]0><
4|\|(|
31|\|8721|\|14|

45 56 45 52 59
54 38 49 4E 47
2C 29 46 4F 52
20 48 12 4C 45
20 54 41 45 20
50 48 45 4E 1F
4D 45 4E 41 4C
2D 52 44 52 4E
52 29 45 20 70 1C
4E 26 45 44 20
4B 45 52 20 45
41 4E 44 20 41
43 52 4F 53 53
20 54 4F 45 20
52 54 52 49 4E
17 55 5E 22 54
42 05 58 20 53
4B 51 4E 14 4S
41 20 54 4A 4S
20 54 48 52 4C
44 45 52 25 47
4F 31 40 20 4F
46 20 41 20 46
4C 4F 43 46 39
4F 16 20 53 57
41 5F 53 29 51
48 41 54 20 51
45 54 54 4C 45
53 20 41 53 20
4F 4E 65 20 4F
4F 44 56 20 4F
4E 54 4F 20 41
20 4C 41 4B 15
7E 10 10 20 20
42 55 54 20C 20
4E 4F 54 20 4F
4E 4C 59 29 51
48 49 53 20C 20
42 41 20 49 53
20 42 49 56 45
4E 20 53 50 45
42 39 41 4C 20
49 4E 53 49 47
48 54 20 49 4C
54 4F 20 32 49
53 54 4F 52 59
3A 20 201C 4B
41 20 44 12 53
45 52 56 45 44
20 54 48 41 54
20 45 41 43 48
20 53 51 52 49
4E 52 20 4B 4F
4E 52 20 40 4F
2C 20 45 41 43
48 20 50 11 52
53 20 13 4E 4E
53 49 53 54 45
4E 47 20 47 46
20 33 31 37 20
59 45 41 52 53
2C 20 31 39 20
32 20 59 45 41
5 13 20 49 1E
20 41 4C 4C 2E
20 41 4E 44 20
41 4C 53 4F 20
51 48 11 54 20
54 48 45 20 51
4F 50 20 52 4F
57 20 4F 4B 20

MAN 41: ...spatial grammar is flattened, given zero-dimensionality, and is stochastic, still, and absolute. That is, Siratori's work cannot offer a mode of *knowing* because the contamination, spectres, viral infections, mutations, and permutations that characterize his work are not syntactically or semantically related through distinct grammatical demarcations; instead Siratori offers an alphanumeric stochastic whole. To *look into* his work is absurd because it does not recognize an *outside; [dies]...*

MAN 42: ...rather, one must continually journey deeper *through* it and where we find that our origins and destinations, causes and effects, temporal bidirections are all, in the end, identical andimmanent. *[dies]...*

\|
|'\3|_471\V17\'
|\|4|'\|'\471\V3
8 0|= 7|-|3 1 9
2 0 8 1 9 4 0
8. 4|\|D (3) 7|-
|3
1|\|73|'\73><7|
_|4|_
|\V|_|L_71\V3|'
\83/|=1|_|\V|1|
|\|4|'\|'\471\V3
8 0|= 7|-|3
|'087|'\V|0|3|'\
|\| 3|'\4
\V\/1773|'\|33|'
\c- 8|_|c-c-3878
7|-|47 7|-|3
|0|'\|73|'\|7 0|=
7|-|383
870|'\138 4|'\3
'|\|4|'\|'\471\V
3 |\V|4|-
|1|\|38° 1|\| 4
'|\|4|'\|'\470|_
0c 1|4|_
|_4|30|'\470|'\\
'' \V/|-|3|'\3
4|_|7|-|0|'\8
4|\|D
|'\34|]3|'\8
1|\|\V3871c-473
{|_|38710|\|8
0|=
73|\V|'|'0|'\4|_1
7\'. |-|1870|'\\.
4|\|D
8|_|3,|3(71\|17
\'. 0|\| 4
|=0|'\|V|4|_
|_3\V3|_| 7|-
|383
|\|4|'\|'\471\V3
8 3|\V|30|]\'
7 1|\V|3
7|'\4\V3|_,
|=0|'\
3><4|\V||'|_3,
\V14 4|3|'\|_||'7
8|'4714|_4|\|D
73|\V|'|'0|'\4|_
[|18|_0(4710|\|
8. 1|\| 8|-
|0|'\7.
|\|4|'\|'\471\V3
8 (4|\| |83
{0|'\|81|]3|'\3|)
1|\V|4c-
1|\|471\V3
7 1|\V|3 |\V|4|-
|4838 0|=
7 1|\V|3-
7|'\4\V3|_
|\|4|'\|'\471\V3
:(1 7|-|3
3\V0|_|_|710|\|
/|_|70|'14|\|
7 1|\V|3-
7|'\4\V3|_
870|'\138 0|=
7|-|3 |_473 1 9
7|-|
{3|\|7|_||'\|'
4|\|D 34|'\|_\'
2 0 7|-|

50 45 47 53 70
49 4E 44 49 41
43 04 95 44 20
49 45 41 50 54
20 57 42 49 41
20 54 46 45 20
45 41 53 54 20
41 49 53 01 49
45 45 44 26 51
48 45 50 55 45
53 43 4C 40 2?
45 45 4E 45 20
54 48 49 29 57
45 42 63 50 41
04 70 54 1? 3V
20 4C 41 57 45
52 20 45 4E 44
20 4E 46 20 51
58 45 20 53 04
52 30 46 47 55
20 49 45 4C 49
45 42 5 E40 44
5V 51 54 20 40
50 06 4E 59 49
54 45 20 20 40
50 45 50 45 4E
51 2C 54 51 54
45 20 5V 53 44
54 2B 41 47 43
41 31 4? 51 4C
57 2C 20 41 5C
41 42 53 2C 2C
53 12 17 54 41
4? 53 5E 16 51
55 51 40 53 2C
20 41 50 04 20
43 4C 5? 40 41
41 55 40 40 41
45 4C 4E 57 2E
57 46 12 12 30
53 49 15 10 45
4? 51 40 40 41
41 4E 53 20 0E
46 20 48 41 54
55 54 42 20 54
55 54 2C 20 54
48 45 20 47 51
55 47 43 53 20
71 30 53 41 20
01 53 40 41 4E
53 53 40 41 40
51 20 20 54 45
45 20 22 43 53
54 54 0C 51 45
54 20 20 5V 4C
54 20 23 53 53
45 20 47 52 41
45 40 40 53 50
46 10 51 45 42
41 53 51 40 53
50 20 54 40 40
41 2C 47 41 51
41 45 42 20 46
11 20 42 53 54
41 41 42 45 41
20 15 41 35 20
11 44 14 65 44
49 4E 45 41 4C
20 53 54 54 40

WOMAN 43: ... "When we say 'chaos,'" as Franco Berardi notes, "we mean two different, complimentary movements. We refer to the swirling of our surrounding semiotic flows, which we receive as if they were 'sound and fury.' But we also refer to attempts to reconcile this encompassing environmental rhythm with our own intimate, internal rhythm of interpretation."[xix] Siratori utters chaos with aDadaist and Mavoist spirit of rage, revulsion, and revolution: *[dies]*...

MAN 43: ...chaos is the intimate, novel interpretation that breathes life into *neutral openness amidst immanence*. This shift from buildingstructures of meaning to building potent modular structures of glitched poetics helps us understand

{3|\|7|_|'\V-{
2}.7|-|3
{[_083|-|_00|"
|"4|"\4[]0><
4|\|[]
31|\|8731|\|14|
\|
|"\3|_171\17\'
|\|4|"\|"\471\/3
8 0|- 7|-|3 1 9
2 08 1 9 4 0
8, 4|\|[] (3|.7|-
|3
1|\|73|"\73>c7|
|4|_
|\/|[_|l_71\/3|'
\83'|=}|_|\/|l|
|\|4|"\|"\471\/3
8-9|= 7|-|3
|"('87|\/|0|}3|"\
|\| 3|"\4
\/\/1773|\|_|33|'
%-8|_|c<-3878
7|-|47 7|-|3
[0|\|73|\|7 0|-
7|-|383
870|"\138 4|"\3
"\|\|4|"\|"\471\/
3 |\/|4|-
|1|\|38" 1|\| 4
"\|\|4|"\|"\170|_
0<-l|41_
|_4|30|"\470|"\\
"' \\/|-|3|"\3
4|_|7|-|0|"\8
4|\|[]
|"\34[]3|"\8
1|\|\/38?|c<-473
[J|_|287|0|\|8
0|=
73|\/|"0|"\4|_1
7\, |-|1829|"\\,
4|\|[]
8|_||3|3(71\/17
\' 0|\| 4
|=0|"\|\/|1|_
|_3\/3|_ 7|-
|383
|\|4|"\|"\471\/3
8 3|\/||89|\"
71|\/|3
7|"\4\/3|_.
|=0|"\
3><4|\/||"|_3-
\/14 4|3|"\|_||"7
8|"474|_ 4|\|[]
73|\/| |"0|"\4|_
[)|8|_0(47|0|\|
3-1|\| 8|-
|0|"\7,
|\|4|"\|"\471\/3
3 {4|\| |33
(0|\|8|}3|"\3[]
1|\/|4<-
1|\|"\71\/3
71|\/|3 |\/|4|-
|4238 0|=
71|\/|3-
7|"\4\/3|_
|\|1|"\|"\171\/3
: { 1 }7|-|3
3\/0|_|_|710|\|
7|_|20|"\14|\|
71|\/|3-
7|"\4\/3|_.

4E 47 3A 20 43
45 54 57 45 45
4E 20 54 48 45
20 59 15 41 51
20 37 38 25 20
54 48 45 20 49
4E 56 41 53 49
48 41 20 41 46
20 54 48 45 20
53 43 49 54 54 48
49 41 4E 53 20
4F 48 20 41 44
49 41 20 53 31
48 41 2E 20 41
4F 48 20 54 45 49
45 20 49 45 45 31
52 20 31 38 32
3D 3014 54 48
45 20 45 41 54
54 18 20 48 41
20 53 54 54 34
49 45 44 20 54
48 45 20 50 48
53 53 49 42 45
4C 49 54 49 45
53 20 1F 46 20
20 4C 47 1F 19
4E 47 20 3F 4E
20 41 4C 20 20
53 45 56 45 1E
20 53 54 52 49
4E 27 52 2E
201D 20 20 41
53 20 51 48 49
52 20 53 4F 1E
47 20 47 49 56
45 53 20 42 4F
54 48 20 18 41
20 41 46 44 20
54 48 45 30 41
50 45 53 20 53
50 45 44 49 43
4C 20 49 4E 53
49 47 48 51 20
19 48 54 41 20
54 45 45 40 45 20
28 57 48 49 43
48 20 46 45 41
4E 53 20 1C 49
54 54 40 45 20
34 47 20 48 41
20 42 55 54 20
49 53 20 50 53
48 47 4E 4F 53
54 49 43 41 51
49 46 45 20 46
48 52 20 54 48
45 20 11 50 49
53 20 20 41 4E
14 20 54 45 4D
50 54 19 40 47
76 95 93 20 51
47 20 54 48 49
4E 48 20 41 42
45 55 54 20 51
48 45 20 59 45
41 52 20 31 39
38 30 2076 29
20 20 57 45 20
53 45 45 20 54
48 45 20 45 4E
47 49 41 1E 45 45
52 20 4F 46 20
54 49 40 45 20
4E 53 41 4E 43

Siratori's writing as a supermodern project. *[dies]*...

WOMAN 44: ...It does not *use* the technical word as such; instead, it expresses the chrono*a*topic liberation of poetic immanence via absolute paradox of chronotopic simultaneity.

[MALE BODYBUILDER and FEMALE BODYBUILDER enter stage]

FEMALE BODYBUILDER: *[posing, flexing, and speaking in unison]* Siratori is a great novelist and has made a more powerful contribution tothe novel for the 21st century than, say, Jonathan Franzen.

[MALE BODYBUILDER and FEMALE BODYBUILDER exit stage; MAN 44 Enters]

870|"\138 0|=
7|-|3 |_473 1 9
7|-|
{3|\|7|_||"\\'
4|\|0 34|"\|_\'
2 0 7|-|
{3|\|7|_||"\\,|
2}7|-|3
{|_023[|-|_00|"
|"4|"\4[0><
4|\|0
31|\|8731|\|14|
\|
|"\3|_471\/17\'
|\|4|"\|"\471\/3
80|= 7|-|3 1 9
2 0 s-1 9 4 0
8.4|\|0 {3|7|-
|3
1|\|73|"\73><7|
_|4|_
|\/|_||_71\/3|"
\83/|=1|_|\/|1[
|\|4|"\|"\471\/3
8 0|= 7|-|3
|"087|\/|0|}3|"\
|\| 3|"\4
\/\/1773|\||33|"
\c- 8|_|<-c-3878
7|-|47 7|-|3
[0|\|73|\|7 0|=
7|-|383
870|"\138 4|"\3
"|\|4|"\|"\471\/
3 |\/|4[|-
{1|\|38° 1|\| 4
"|\|4|"\|"\470|_
0c-1[4|_
|_4|30|"\470|"\\
"' \/\/|-|3|"\3
4|_|7|-|0|"\8
4|\|0
|"\34|}3|"\8
1|\|\/3871c-473
{,}|_|38710|\|8
0|=
73|\/|"0|"\4|_1
7\', |-|1870|"\\.
4|\|0
8|_||3,|3{71\/17
\'_0|\| 4
|=0|"\|\/|4|_
|_3\/3|_, 7|-
|383
|\|4|"\|"\471\/3
8 3|\/||30D\'
7|\/|3
7|"\4\/3|_,
|=0|"\
3><4|\/||"|_3,
\/14 4|3|"\|_||"7
8|"47|4|_ 4|\|0
73|\/|"0|"\4|_
{|18|_0{4710|\|
8. 1|\| 8|-
|0|"\7.
|\|4|"\|"\471\/3
8 {4|\| |33
{0|\|31|}3|"\3|0
1|\/|4c-
1|\|471\/3
7|\/|3 |\/|4[|-
|4838 0|=
7|\/|3-
7|"\4\/3|_,

MAN 44: ...Mikhail Bakhtin writes that "the study of the novel as a genre is distinguished by peculiar difficulties...due to the unique nature of the object itself: the novel is the sole genre that continues to develop, that is as yet uncompleted"[xx] It is on this formalist point—the novel as an incomplete object—where Siratori makes his biggest contribution. *[dies]*...

WOMAN 45: ...A novel is not a receptacle for an exhaustive and complete study of its subject matter. Instead, it is a glitching, mutating, and permutating formalist vortex, without content, beyond-sense (заумь), infinite in its accreting towards zero, an object as objection to conventionality. His glitch poetics and *[dies]*...

WOMAN 46: ...granular writing is

the embodiment of *form
mutating and permutating*
having shed their semantic
exuviae: it is a neutral and
restless incompletion in infinite
process. So, what of the atomic
or fundamental processes that
underly granular writing and
glitch poetics? *[dies]*...

MAN 45: ...What is one wishes
to—rather than engage directly
with the formalism of granularity
and glitch—offer visual, concrete
textualizations of the
technological word as such?
[dies]...

*[LEAD ACROBAT and his POSSE
OF ACROBATS enter stage left]*

LEAD ACROBAT: *[with an
announcer's finest diaphragm-
supported vibrato]* Here we turn
to the patamathematical poem.
Rather than foregrounding the

incongruity between content and form in the supermodern era as an act of poetic insurgency, the patamathematical poem wishes to stick even closer toKhlebnikov and Kruchenykh's nonrepresentational word as such. That is, the poetry itself *is* the technical word: it offers the atomic unit of technical poetics *as* the work itself. For example, consider the following patamathematical poem enacting theprocessualism of the word "before":

[LEAD ACROBAT and POSSE OF ACROBATS proceed to clamber on top of one another shouting "allez, hop" to form the precise shape of the following patamathematical poem]

4F 50 20 52 4E
57 20 4F 46 20
50 45 47 53 20
49 41 14 49 46
41 54 45 44 20
59 45 41 52 53
20 57 13 45 4E
70 54 45 15 20
45 41 53 54 20
41 54 53 41 49
44 45 43 70 51
48 45 20 57 45
53 54 2C 29 57
45 49 40 45 20
51 45 15 70 50
45 47 53 20 41
54 20 54 48 45
20 4C 4F 57 45
51 20 45 4E 41
20 41 46 20 56
4D 45 20 53 54
6 49 45 47 53
20 49 4F 44 49
45 41 54 45 44
20 41 45 20 4F
50 50 1F 53 48
5A 45 20 4D 4F
5b 45 4D 45 45
54 2C 20 54 48
45 20 57 15 53
54 70 41 47 41
49 4E 53 54 20
54 48 45 20 45
41 53 54 2E 20
49 4F 54 54 48
45 20 54 4F 5B
20 52 3F 57 20
57 45 53 45 20
54 48 45 20 56
41 3E 44 41 4C
53 2C 20 11 52
41 47 53 2C 20
54 41 52 54 41
52 53 2C 20 54
5b 52 48 53 7C
26 43 48 44 20
47 45 52 4D 41
4E 53 3B 20 42
45 4C 45 52 20
57 45 52 45 20
54 48 45 20 45
47 59 50 54 49
41 4E 53 20 4F
46 20 48 41 54
53 48 2E 20 53
55 54 2C 20 54
48 45 20 17 57
45 45 18 53 29
4F 15 26 41 44
56 52 53 15 55
53 2C 20 54 45
45 20 54 49 5A
54 48 48 49 41 4E
53 2C 20 54 48
45 20 47 52 45
45 48 53 20 4F
46 20 50 45 52
49 43 4C 15 53
25 20 54 48 45
20 52 4F 4D 41
4E 53 2E 20 4E
41 20 11 54 54
41 43 45 45 44
20 4F 4E 45 20
41 34 44 49 54

$$\frac{-b \pm \sqrt{b^{before^2} - Before}}{2a \frac{\partial y}{\partial x}\sqrt{a^2 + b^2}e^3\sqrt[3]{before}°F\Delta R \ni^{-i\omega t} \Lambda_e^b \, 44}$$

$$\iiint_b^{before} 4$$

$$\ll \Delta \gg (before) = \begin{cases} -x, & x < \blacksquare \\ x, & x \geq \blacksquare \end{cases}$$

$$\frac{b}{e}$$
$$f$$
$$o\sqrt{o + o^2}$$
$$r$$

$$\frac{-b \pm \sqrt{b^{\frac{\partial y}{\partial x}^2} - 4a\frac{\delta y}{\delta x}c}}{2b}$$

$$\frac{e}{f}$$
$$o$$
$$r$$

$$\frac{-b \pm \sqrt{e^2 - 0b4}}{2a \oint\!\!\oint\!\!\oint^{\,^n_1 \gamma}} \qquad 0$$

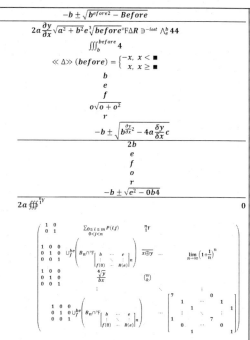

[LEAD ACROBAT and POSEE OF ACROBATS disassemble, line-up, bow to audience]

LEAD ACROBAT: And, as a further example, what of the following patamathematical piece allowing the preposition "from" to reveal that, as a technical word, it does not operate via logical relations, but

7|°\4\/3|_
|=0|°\
3><4|\/|1°|_3,
\/14 4|3|°\|_|1°7
8|°4714|_4|\|[)
73|\/|1°0|°\41_
|)18|_0(4710|\|
8. 1|\| 8|-
|0|°\7,
|\|4|°\|°\471\/3
8 (4|\| |83
{0|\|81|)3|°\3[)
1|\/|4c-
1|\|4|°\471\/3
71|\/|3 1\/|4(|-
|483 8 0|=
71|\/|3-
7|°\4\/3|_
|\|4|°\|°\471\/3
:(1] ?|-|3
3\/0|_|_|710|\|
/|_|70|°14|\|
71|\/|3-
7|°\4\/3|_
870|°\138 0|=
7|-|3 |_473 1 9
7|-|
(3|\|7|_|1°\'
4|\|[) 34|°\|_\'
2 07|-|
(3|\|7|_|1°\'. (
2] 7|-|3
(|_083|)-|_00|°
|°4|°\4|)0><
4|\|[)
31|\|8721|\|14|
\|
|°\3|_471\/17\'
|\|4|°\|°\471\/3
8 0|= 7|-|3 1 9
2 08-1 9 4 0
8, 4|\|[)·(3 | 7|-
|3
1|\|73|°\73><7|
_|4|_
|\/|_|1_71\/3|°
\83/|=1|_|\/|1(
|\|4|°\|°\471\/3
8 0|= 7|-|3
|°087|\/|0|)3|°\
|\| 3|°\4.
\/\/1773|\|33|°
\c- 8|_|c-c-3278
7|-|47 7|-|3
{0|\|73|\|7 0|=
7|-|383
870|°\138 4|°\3
°|\|4|°\|°\471\/
3 |\/|4(|-
|1|\|38° 1|\| 4
°|\|4|°\|°\470|_
0c-|(4|_
|_4|30|°\470|°\\
"· \/\/|-|3|°\3
4|_|7|-|0|°\8
4|\|[)
|°\34|)3|°\8
1|\|\/\/387 1c-473
(.)|_|38710|\|8
0|=
73|\/|1°0|°\4|_1
7\', |-|1270|°\|\/,
4|\|[)
8|_|(3,|3(71\/17
\'. 0|\| 4

in itself at the atomic level making possible its appearance as a processual term: *"allez, hop!"*

*[*LEAD ACROBAT *and* POSSE OF ACROBATS *proceed to clamber on top of one another shouting "allez, hop!" to form the precise shape of the follow patamathematical poem]*

$$\int_{-\infty}^{\infty} r^{-om^2} from = \left[\int_{-\infty}^{\infty} r^{-om^2} from \int_{-\infty}^{\infty} r^{-om^2} from\right]^{1/2}$$

$$= \left[\int_0^{2\pi}\int_{-\infty}^{\infty} r^{-om^2} from\right]^{1/2}$$

$$= \left[\pi\int_0^r m^{-fr} om \int_{-\infty}^{\infty} r^{-om^2} from\right]^{f(r)/o(m)}$$

$$= \sqrt{\pi} from$$

$$\coprod_{fr} fr \sum_{\substack{f\le r\le o<m \\ f<r<o<m}} o(m,m)\,\langle f|r|o(m)\rangle \bigwedge_f \begin{pmatrix} f & \cdots & r \\ \vdots & \ddots & \vdots \\ o & \cdots & \mathbf{M}\end{pmatrix}$$

$$\int_{-\infty}^{\infty} r^{-om^2} from = \left[\int_{-\infty}^{\infty} r^{-om^2} from \int_{-\infty}^{\infty} r^{-om^2} from\right]^{1/2}$$

$$= \left[\int_0^{2\pi}\int_{-\infty}^{\infty} r^{-om^2} from\right]^{1/2} \, {}^f_r(om) f \therefore r \quad O \quad m$$

$$= \left[\pi\int_0^r m^{-fr} om \int_{-\infty}^{\infty} r^{-om^2} from\right]^{f(r)/o(m)}$$

$$= \sqrt{\pi from} \coprod_{fr} fr \sum_{\substack{f\le r\le om \\ f<r<o<m}} o(m,m)\,\langle f|r|o(m)\rangle \bigwedge_f \begin{pmatrix} f & \cdots & r \\ \vdots & \ddots & \vdots \\ o & \cdots & \mathbf{M}\end{pmatrix}$$

$$\coprod_{fr} fr \sum_{\substack{f\le r\le om \\ f<r<o<m}} o(m,m)\,\langle f|r|o(m)\rangle \bigwedge_f \begin{pmatrix} f & \cdots & r \\ \vdots & \ddots & \vdots \\ o & \cdots & \mathbf{M}\end{pmatrix} =$$

$$= \left[\int_0^{2\pi}\int_{-\infty}^{\infty} r^{-om^2} from\right]^{1/2}$$

$$= \left[\pi\int_0^r m^{-fr} om \int_{-\infty}^{\infty} r^{-om^2} from\right]^{f(r)/o(m)}$$

$$= \sqrt{\pi from} \coprod_{fr} fr \sum_{\substack{f\le r\le om \\ f<r<o<m}} o(m,m)\,\langle f|r|o(m)\rangle \bigwedge_f \begin{pmatrix} f & \cdots & r \\ \vdots & \ddots & \vdots \\ o & \cdots & \mathbf{M}\end{pmatrix}$$

51 49 40 45 20
4E 55 41 4E 43
44 4E 47 20 48
49 53 20 50 4F
45 52 49 41 20
45 52 41 46 54
2C 20 53 45 45
44 49 41 47 20
41 20 53 45 56
4E 4E 54 43 20
52 54 52 49 4E
47 20 54 4F 52
47 35 4E 45 52
41 51 45 20 50
41 54 20 46 55
51 54 48 45 52
20 49 4E 51 49
47 45 51 20 45
4E 51 46 20 58
40 53 20 67 53
41 40 45 20 50
52 46 44 45 54 45
54 71 20 49 70
57 31 48 54 20
54 41 20 43 40
41 51 48 46 59
20 54 46 41 53
20 54 48 49 52
30 48 51 4E
2039 54 20 51
48 45 20 53 41
40 45 20 45 51
20 201C 4D 41
47 49 43 2010
20 43 48 20 46
41 4E 54 41 53
59 20 3E 4F 56
45 4C 53 20 47
55 54 20 45 53
20 49 4E 53 54
45 41 46 20 41
20 48 49 4F 44
20 3F 46 20 4E
55 40 45 52 4F
29 45 53 59 40
4E 4C 4E 42 49
43 41 3C 20 47
41 1D 45 20 54
48 41 54 20 41
1E 46 45 45 54
53 20 48 41 52
52 41 54 49 56
45 20 53 1F 52
4C 44 53 20 43
4E 44 2C 20 4B
42 4C 45 42 4E
49 4B 4F 56 20
47 44 50 40 40
55 45 44 2C 20
57 4F 55 4C 44
20 45 56 48 4E
56 51 41 1C 4E
50 20 42 55 20
55 53 45 44 20
54 5F 20 12 18
41 4F 42 45 20
41 4C 44 20 30
41 53 54 15 57
20 53 50 41 42
45 54 49 40 45
20 49 54 53 45
4C 46 29 28 49
28 45 2E 2C 20
48 48 40 45 42
4E 45 1B 4F 56

[LEAD ACROBAT and POSEE OF ACROBATS disassemble, line-up, bow to audience, die...MAN 46 enters stage right]

MAN 46: ...What the patamathematical poem *enters* accomplishes is an explicit confrontation with the foundational operations that make the technical word possible. Rather than a rigid transliteration of the word-processed code itself, the patamathematical poem offers [dies]...

WOMAN 47: ...the neutral processes that function without semantic criteria. To interfere and to offer the imaginative is less a corrective than a confluence of agency and processualism: the

0|=
73|\V||'0|'\4|_1
7\', |-|1870|'\\,
4|\|[)
8|_|:3.|3(71\V17
\'.0|\| 4
|=0|'\|V|\4|_
|_3\V3|_.71-
|383
|\|4|'\|'\471\V3
8 3|\V|)30[)\'
71|\V|3
7|'\4\V3|_.
|=0|'\
3>=<4|\V||'|_3.
\V14 4|3|'\|_||'7
2|-'47|4|_.4|\|[)
73|\V||'0|'\4|_
[|18|_0(4710|\|
8. 1|\| 8|-
|0|'\7.
|\|4|'\|'\471\V3
3 (4|\| |33
(0|\|8|])3|'\3()
1|\V|4c-
1|\|471\V3
71|\V|3 |\V|4(|-
|4838.0|=
71|\V|3-
7|'\4\V3|_
|\|4|'\|'\471\V3
:{1}7|-|3
3\V0|_|_|710|\|
/|_|70|'\4|\|
71|\V|3-
7|'\4\V3|_
870|'\138 0|=
7|-|3 |_473 1 9
7|-|
(3|\|7|_||'\'
4|\|[) 34|'\|_\'
2 07|-|
(3|\|7|_||'_(
2)7|-|3
(|_083|]-|_00|'
|'4| '\4[)0><
4|\|[)
31|\|8731|\|14|
\|
|'\3|_471\V17\'
|\|4|'\|'\471\V3
8.0|= 7|-|3 1 9
2 08-1 9 4 0
8. 4|\|[) {3| 7|-
|3
1|\|73|'\73>=<7|
_|4|_
|V|_|_||_71\V3|'
\83/|=1|_|V|1(
|\|4|'\|'\471\V3
8.0|= 7|-|3
|'087|\V|0|)3|'\
|\| 3|'\4.
\V\V1773\\|33|'
\c-8|_|c-c-3872
7|-|47 7|-|3-
|0|\|73|\|7 0|=
7|-|383
870|'\138 4|'\3
'|\|4|'\|'\471\V
3 |\V|4(|-
|1|\|38' 1|\| 4
'|\|4|'\|'\470|_
0c-1[4|_
|_4|30|'\470|'\\

patamathematical poem *is* the technical word as such. It does not signify but *is* the work of art *and* the technical expression upon which it radiates. Just as *[dies]*...

MAN 47: ...the Cubo-Futurists and Dadaists captured the process of random reassembling as resistance, the digital era of the 1980s onward demands engagement with the interfaces that govern the narratives of supermodern life. Granular synthesis and patamathematical poetry aim *[dies]*...

WOMAN 48: ...to *[dies]*...

MAN 48: ...continue this...*[dies]*...

WOMAN 49: ...resistance in the computer-era but, eschews *[dies]*...

52 4F 4D 20 45
56 45 52 20 48
41 50 50 45 4E
49 4E 47 2E 20
45 56 45 52 59
54 48 49 3E 47
2C 20 46 4F 52
"9 48 46 1C 45
2B 54 48 45 20
50 48 45 4E 4F
49 45 4E 41 46
20 57 4F 52 4C
44 3A 20 20 1C
53 48 45 20 4D
4F 56 4A 44 2D
45 35 52 20 48
41 4E 4A 20 40
43 52 4F 55 53
C9 54 45 45 20
53 54 52 29 4F
47 53 3B 20 54
48 45 59 20 53
4F 53 41 44 40
44 20 54 4B 45
20 54 48 53 4E
44 45 52 20 4E
46 46 4D 20 46
46 20 41 70 46
4C 4F 42 48 20
4F 44 20 53 57
4F 4F 59 20 5A
4A 41 55 70 53
35 54 54 4C 45
53 20 41 53 20
4F 4F 48 20 42
4F 44 20 53 2D
4E 54 4F 45 20
4E 54 4F 48 45
4E 54 20 48 48
53 34 4F 52 55
3A 20 20 1C 4B
41 20 2E 42 53
45 52 56 45 11
20 54 48 41 54
20 41 4B 43 48
20 53 34 5A 48
43 47 20 33 4F
4E 53 49 54 54
45 53 40 54 64
45 41 20 4F 46
50 41 52 54 43
2C 20 45 41 48
42 20 20 41 52
54 20 43 4F 11
53 45 20 33 48
4E 37 20 4F 46
20 33 31 27 20
59 46 41 52 54
2C 20 31 39 30
32 20 53 35 41
57 53 73 49 41
29 41 4C 4C 2E
20 41 4E 54 20
41 4C 53 4F 20

MAN 49: ...postmodern pop in favour of *[dies]*...

WOMAN 50: ...a kind of supermodernist transcendence. The rogue individualism of the Cubo-Futurists, Dadaists, beatniks, and punks, it should be noted, can today be easily modeled and predicted by SiliconValley or Shenzhen in the 21stcentury. Xenakis' granular synthesis, Siratori's glitch poetics, and patamathematical poetry, however, aims to resist this by engaging with a kind of *technical* mathe-musico- poetry that creates a state of mind akin to stochastic agency, rather than neoliberal faux individualism. *[dies]*...

MAN 50: ...If, for example, music is "pure expression" (as both

"|\|4|'\|'\471\V
3 |\V|\4[|-
|1|\|38" 1|\| 4
"|\|4|'\|'\470|_
0c-1{4|_
|_4l30|'\470|'\
"\VI-|3|'\3
4|_|7|-|0|'\8
4|\|[]
|'\34[]3|'\8
1|\|\V38716<473
(.)|_|38710|\|8
0|=
73|\V|'\0|'\4|_1
7\'. |-|1870|'\\'.
4|\|[]
8|_|l3,l3(7l\V|17
\V.0|\| 4
|=0|'\|\V|4|_
|_3\V3|_7|-
|383
|\|4|'\|'\471\V3
83|\V|l|30[\|'
71|\V|3
7|'\4\V3|_
|=0|'\
3><4|\V||'\|_3,
\V14 4l3|'\|_||'7
8|'\47|4|_ 4|\|[]
73|\V|'\0|'\4|_
|]18|_0(4710|\|
8. 1|\| 8|-
|0|'\7,
|\|4|'\|'\471\V3
8{4|\| i33
{0|\|81[]3|'\3[]
1|\V|4c-
1|\|471\V3
71|\V|3 |\V|4[|=
-|4838 0|=
71|\V|3-
7|'\4\V3|_
|\|4|'\|'\471\V3
:{ 1} 7|-|3
3\V0|_|_|710|\|
7|_|70|'14|\|
71|\V|3-
7|'\4\V3|_
870|'\138 0|=
7|-|3 |_473 1 9
7|-|
{3|\|7|_||'\\'
4|\|[| 31|'\|_\'
2 07|-|
{3|\|7|_||'\\'.{
2}7|-|3
(|_083|]-|_00|"
|'4|'\4[]0><
4|\|[]
31|\|873l|\|14|
\|
|'\3|_471\V17\'
|\|4|'\|'\471\V3
8 0|= 7|-|3 1 9
2 08-1 9 4 0
8, 4|\|[]{3|7|-
|3
1|\|73|'\73><7|
_|4|_
|\V|_||_71\V3|'
\83'|=1|_|\V|1[
|\|4|'\|'\471\V3
8 0|=7|-|3
|'087|\V|0[]3|'\
|\| 3|'\4.

54.46.41.56.20
54.48.45.26.54
45.50.20.57.4f
57.50.41.56.20
57.45.47.50.70
49.4f.41.47.45
41.53.45.50.20
57.45.11.57.45
70.57.49.44.4f
20.56.45.15.20
79.47.45.53.70
41.54.54.41.43
46.45.44.20.54
48.45.20.57.45
54.43.77.20.54
38.45.30.65.70
54.48.45.20.50
45.47.53.20.45
41.20.57.48.45
70.30.45.57.45
57.30.45.30.44
55.39.45.3f.44
20.41.30.30.54
47.55.20.20.41
54.45.46.45.52
30.49.45.44.46
44.41.54.15.41
30.47.45.20.41
55.50.45.39.41
54.45.20.40.47
56.42.49.45.4f
30.75.40.54.48
54.20.53.45.52
54.20.41.47.41
70.4f.53.54.20
48.45.20.20.44
51.47.45.70.51
45.42.53.20.20
54.57.50.54.45
57.20.40.45.20
44.52.40.54.48
45.52.45.20.45
54.40.41.53.20
57.45.53.20.45
30.44.45.20.20
41.46.55.20.4f
48.20.48.31.54
54.45.15.50.53
55.55.52.50.54
48.45.20.47.52
45.45.40.53.20
48.45.70.4f.41
48.45.52.45.41
53.20.20.53.38
45.20.55.45.70
54.48.15.50.24
45.50.70.52.4f
53.30.41.48.20
40.45.30.54.49
45.54.53.64.24
41.53.54.11.42

Flusser and Xenakis hold) then hacking the technological apparatus of music production to produce "impossible" sonic textures characterized by their unpredictability and latent potentialities may enhance or accelerate pure expression against the algorithmic determinism characteristic of the early *[dies]*...

WOMAN 51: ...21st century. Khlebnikov's overall project, like all utopian projects, is ill-conceived.Crystalizing all of time and space into a manageableand modular chronotope is not only an impossible and absurd idea it is a bad idea. After all, *[dies]*...

MAN 51: ...who's going to author it? *[dies]*...

MAN 52: ...Now we are left asking, how might the technical

\\V|773|\\|33|\"
\c-3|_|c-c.3278
7|-|47.7|-|3
|0|\|73|\|7.0|=
7|-|383
870|\138.4|\3
\|\|4|\|\471V
3.|\|3\|-
|1\\|38\" 1|\|.4
\|\|4|\|\470|_
.0c-1|4|_
|_4|30|\470|\\
\" V\|-|3|\|3
4|_|7|-|0|\8
4|\|[|
|\34|03|\8
1|\|\387|c-473
\3|_|387|0|\|8
.0|=
73|\V||\0|\4|_|
7_| |1870|\\\.
4|\|[|
8|_|[6|3\7|V1\\
Y.0|\| 4
|=0|\|V|4|_
|_3\V3|_.7|-
|383
|\|4|\|\471V3
.8.3|\V|00|\
73|\V|3
7|\4\2|_
|=0|\\
3><4|\V|\"|_3.
\V14.4|3|\\|_|\"7
8|\471.4|_4|\|[|
73|\V|\"0|\"4|_
[|18|_.0|47|0|\|
.8. 1|\| 8|-
|0|\7.
|\|4|\|\471V3
.7.|1|\| 83
|0|\|8|[|3|\"\2[|
1|\|4<
1|\|471V3
7|\|V|3 |\V|4|-
|4538.0|=
73|\V|3
7|\4\2|_
|\|4|\|\471V3
.|1.1|7|-|9
3\/0|_1._|710|\|
.7|_|70|\"14|\|
73|\V|3-
.7|\4\2|_
870|\138.0|=
7|-|3.|_.473.1.9
7|-|
[3|\|7|_|\"\\"
4|\|[|.34|\"\|_\\"
.2.0.7|-|
[3|\V|_|\"\\.1
.2.|.7|-|4
[|_0370|-|_00|\"
|\"4|.\"4|[|0><
4|\|[|
33|\|\373|.|\|14|
.\|
|\"\3|_.473\V17\"
[\|4|\|\471V3
.8.0|= 7|.|3.1.9
.2.0<-7.9.4.0
.8.4|\|[|(3|.7|-
.|3
1|\|73|\"\73><3\"
_|4|_

48 45 44 20 54
42 35 20 57 45
53 51 2C 20 57
48 49 4C 45 20
54 48 45 20 50
45 47 53 20 41
54 20 51 48 45
C6 52 45 57 45
52 20 45 4E 44
20 4F 46 20 54
48 15 20 52 53
52 45 4E 47 53
20 39 4E 44 19
43 41 54 15 41
20 41 4E 20 41
50 50 41 51 54
54 45 20 40 4F
56 15 40 15 4C
54 2C 20 54 48
45 20 52 45 5
54 20 41 47 41
45 10 53 54 20
53 45 35 20 45
41 53 54 2C 20
49 4C 20 53 45
45 20 54 4E 50
20 52 4E 57 20
57 45 52 45 70
54 35 45 20 56
41 4C 44 41 4C
53 20 20 41 5
41 42 53 2C 20
54 41 52 54 41
52 53 27 20 54
55 52 48 54 2C
20 41 4E 44 20
47 45 52 4D 41
4E 53 38 20 47
45 4C 4F 57 52
57 45 52 45 20
54 48 45 20 45
47 50 50 44 49
41 4E 53 20 41
16 20 48 41 54
53 45 15 50 53
55 51 2C 20 54
48 45 20 4F 52
45 45 48 52 20
4F 46 20 4E 54
59 53 53 45 55
53 2C 20 54 48
54 48 45 20 57
4F 50 20 52 4F
57 20 4F 46 20
50 45 47 53 20
49 4E 45 69 43
41 51 45 14 20
59 49 41 52 32
29 57 4N 45 4E
20 53 48 45 29
45 31 53 54 20
41 54 4E 41 41
45 45 44 20 54
48 35 20 57 45
53 51 2C 20 5
44 49 4C 45 29
54 48 45 20 50
45 47 53 20 41
54 20 56 4F 45
20 4C 4F 57 45
52 20 45 4E 44
20 4F 46 20 54
48 45 20 52 53
52 48 48 47 52
20 33 4E 44 49

word as such offer a way forward? Is the technological neutrality of immanent mathe-musico- poetry subject to the same Abrahamic eschatological biases or Russian Cosmism's anthropocentric teleology? In his early life, *[dies]*...

WOMAN 52: ...Khlebnikov would be passionately political and supportive of the revolution. Yet, as certain Russian Futurists became increasingly politically active, Khlebnikov's eccentricities would have him desperately scrambling to discover a solution that might revise the historical oscillations of slaughter and prevent them altogether. He was a poet and a scholar, and ill-equipped to become are volitionary. He remained in support of both the October and February Revolutions, *[dies]*...

|V|_||_71V3|'
\83/|=1|_|V|1(
|\|4|'|'471V3
8 0|= 7|-|3
|'087|V|0|]3|'\
|\| 3|'\,1
VV1773|\|.33|'
\c-8|_|c-c-5878
7|-|47 7|-|3
|0|\|73|\|7 0|=
7|-|383
870|'\138 4|'\3
'|\|4|'\|'\471V
3 |V|4(|-
|1|\|33' 1|\| 4
'|\|4|'\|'\470|_
0c-1|4|_
|_4|30|'\470|'\\
'' VV/|-|3|'\3
4|_|7|-|0|'\8
4|\|[]
|'\34|]3|'\8
1|\|V3871c-473
(,|_|38710|\|8
0|=
73|V||'0|'\4|_1
7\', |-|1870|'\\',
4|\|[]
8|_|i.3.|3(71V17
\' 0|\| 4
|=0|'\|V|4|_
|_3V3|_. 7|-
|383
|\|4|'\|'\471V3
8 3|V||30|\'
71|V|3
7|'\4V3|_,
|=0|'\
3>c4|V||'|_3,
\/14 4|3|'\|_||'7
8|'4714|_ 4|\|[]
73|V||'0|'\4|_
(]18|_0(4710|\|
8. 1|\| 8|-
|0|'\7.
|\|4|'\|'\471V3
8 (4|\| |33
(0|\|81|]3|'\3[]
1|V|4c-
1|\|471V3
71|\|V|3 |V|4(|-
|4828 0|=
71|V|3-
7|'\4V3|_
|\|4|'\|'\471V3
:(1|7|-|3
3\V0|_|_|710|\|
/|_|70|'14|\|
71|\|V|3-
7|'\4V3|_
870|'\138 0|=
7|-|3 |_473. 1 9
7|-|
(3|\|7|_||'\'
4|\|[] 34|'\|_\'
2 07|-|
(3|\|7|_||'\'. (
2 17|-|3
(|_083|]-|_00|'
|'4|'\4[]0><
4|\|[]
31|\|8731|\|14|_
\|
|'\3|_471V17\'
'\|4|'\|'\471V3

MAN 53: ...and, rather than a decorated soldier, he helped organize nature reserves in the Volga delta with his father. In his later years, Khlebnikov would frequently fall into wandering, homelessness, and malnutrition. In 1919, *[dies]*...

MAN 54: ...the city of Kharkov, where he was at the time, was captured by the White Army; Khlebnikov narrowly escaped prison or conscription by feigning madness and seeking safe haven in an asylum. He was then to realize that, once you've convinced the psychiatric establishment that you are mad, it is *very hard* to convince them that you aren't. *[dies]*...

WOMAN 53: ...In other words, it took him some time to argue his way *out* of the asylum. *[dies]*...

20 52 4F 57 20
57 35 52 45 20
54 48 45 20 56
41 4F 4C 41 4C
53 2C 20 20 41 52
41 42 53 2C 20
54 41 52 54 41
53 53 2C 20 20 51
55 52 48 53 25
20 41 4E 44 20
47 45 52 40 41
48 53 4E 20 43
45 4C 4F 57 20
57 45 52 15 20
51 48 35 20 45
47 53 50 54 41
41 4E 53 20 4F
46 20 12 41 54
54 48 49 50 33
55 54 2C 20 50
45 35 25 47 52
05 45 46 53 20
4F 46 20 4F 44
50 53 53 05 55
53 2C 20 54 45
54 48 15 20 54
4F 50 20 57 4F
57 20 4F 45 20
50 35 47 53 20
49 4C 44 49 44
41 54 35 41 20
53 45 41 52 53
20 57 48 45 4E
20 54 48 45 20
45 41 41 54 20
41 54 54 41 20
48 45 44 20 54
48 45 20 57 45
53 54 20 20 57
42 49 4C 45 20
54 48 45 20 50
44 47 53 20 41
54 20 54 45 20
20 4C 4F 57 45
52 20 15 1E 44
20 3F 46 20 53
38 45 20 50 54
52 49 4E 47 53
20 49 41 74 49
41 41 54 45 44
20 41 4E 20 4F
50 50 4F 52 44
51 35 20 40 4F
54 45 40 45 4E
54 50 20 54 42
45 20 57 45 48
54 20 20 54 54
45 20 50 54 45
53 20 23 20 54
55 52 45 53 25
20 41 1E 44 20
47 45 52 40 41
4E 53 3E 20 42
45 4C 4F 4F 57 20

WOMAN 54: ...When Khlebnikov returned to the Volga valley in1921, he would witness the horrible Volga famine. He would die not too long after in June 1922at the young age of 36 after years of malnutrition, bouts of typhus, and malaria. Shortly afterwards, his work would undergo increasing censorship, and the word as such (and its technical progeny) would rest dormant. Khlebnikov's work sought to experience space-time as a totality to understand the whole and, if possible, engineer history. One way of thinking about the obscured trajectory of Khlebnikov's work may offer unique methodologies and stylistics for narratives that deal with the trauma of history. *[dies]*...

MAN 55: ...Indeed, perhaps this is a time to start thinking of the

"|\|4|'\|'\471\|'
3 |\|4[|-
|1|\|38" 1|\| 4
"|\|4|'\|'\470|_
0c-1(4|_
|_4|30|'\470|'\\
"'\/|-|3|'\3
4|_|7|-|0|'\8
4|\|[]
|'\34|]3|'\8
1|\|\|/3871c-473
{}|_|38710|\|8
0|=
73|\/|{'0|'\3|_1
7\'. |-|1870|'\\'.
4|\|[]
8|_|]3,|3|71\/|'17
\'. 0|\| 1
|=0|'\|\/|4|_
|_3\/3|_ 7|-
|383
|\|4|'\|'\471\/3
8 3|\/|]30[]\'
71|\/|3
7|'\4\/3|_
|=0|'\
3><4|\/|'|'|_3,
\/14 4|3|'\|_||'7
8|'4714|_ 4|\|[]
73|\/|'|'0|'\4|_
[]18|_0{4710|\|
8. 1|\| 8|-
|0|'\7,
|\|4|'\|'\471\/3
8 [4|\| |33
{0|\|81[]3|'\3[]}
1|\/|4c-
1|\|'\471\/3
71|\/|3 |\/|4{|-
|4838 0|=
71|\/|3-
7|'\4\/3|_
|\|4|'\|'\471\/3
:{1}7|-|3
3\/0|_|_|7109|\|
/|_|70|'14|\|
71|\/|3-
7|'\4\/3|_
87'0|'\138 0|=
7|-|3 |_473 1 9
7|-|
{3|\|7|_||'\'
4|\|[] 34|'\|_\'
2 07|-|
{3|\|7|_||'\\. {
2}?|-|3
{|_083|]-|_00|'
|'4|'\4[]0><
4|\|[]
31|\|8731|\|14|
\|
|'\3|_471\/17\'
|\|4|'\|'\471\/3
8 0|= 7|-|3 1 9
2 0 8-1 9 4 0
8, 4|\|[] {3}7|-
|3
1|\|73|'\73><7|
_|4|_
|\/|_||_71\/3|'
\83/|=1|_|\/|1(
|\|4|'\|'\471\/3
8 0|= 7|-|3
|'087|\/|0[]3|'\
|\| 3|'\4.

value that formalist, experimental narratives may offer into processes of grief and volatile, intrusive memories. *[dies]...*

WOMAN 55: ...All attempts to manage these things away are futile, and perhaps it is best to accept this as a way forward. Rather than defeatist, what we can carry with us today is the reminder that Khlebnikov's formalist time-travel makes sense of a tragic past and seeks to engineer a future of beauty, transrational compassion, and peace through art is not necessarily a goal that can be achieved through nostalgia, but a task that should remain central to an ethics of life-as-innovative-art. If the word as such was the foundation for this failed project, *[dies]...*

4F 50 20 52 4F
57 20 4F 48 20
58 45 47 53 20
47 41 44 45 43
41 54 45 44 20
59 45 41 52 53
20 57 48 45 4C
'59 54 48 43 20
45 41 53 84 20
41 54 53 41 43
48 48 41 20 51
53 54 2C 20 52
'58 49 4C 45 20
51 43 45 20 58
45 42 53 20 41
54 20 54 58 45
20 4C 45 57 45
5 20 45 4E 44
20 4F 46 20 54
48 45 20 53 54
42 49 4E 12 53
20 49 20 44 49
47 41 54 45 44
20 41 4E 20 4F
50 50 4F 53 49
58 45 20 4D 42
56 45 4D 15 4E
54 2C 20 54 48
45 20 57 45 53
54 00 11 07 41
49 4E 53 54 2D
5J 48 45 20 45
41 53 54 2E 20
49 3F 70 54 48
45 20 54 4F 5O
20 53 4F 57 20
57 45 53 4J 20
54 48 45 20 56
41 4E 44 41 4C
53 2C 20 20 11 52
41 47 59 3C 2A
54 41 52 54 41
52 53 2C 20 54
55 51 48 53 2C
20 41 4E 44 20
20 54 48 45 20
15 41 53 54 20
11 54 41 41 43
48 45 44 20 51
48 45 20 57 45
53 54 2C 20 52

MAN 56: ...then perhaps the technical word as such may offer insight into a reformulated substratum uponwhich to build a new granular, aleatoric, and patamathematical poetics of insurgency for the 21st century. Rather than engineer the universe as a whole, why not rewrite the universe by remodeling the non-objective, anti-representational supermodern reality from the neutral, processual substratum uponwhich it radiates. *[dies]*...

[Pause. Silence. MALE BODYBUILDER enters stage left and pulls curtain towards the close position. Simultaneously, FEMALE BODYBUILDER enter stage right pulling the curtain towards the close position. When curtain is closed, they both perform front double biceps pose].

7|-|383
870|\138 4|\3
"|\|4|"\|"\471V
3 |V|4(-
|1|\|38" 1|\| 4
"|\|4|"\|"\470|_
0(-1(1|_
|_4|30|"\470|"\\
'" VV|-|3|"\3
4|_|7|-|0|"\8
4|\|[]
|"\34[]3|"\8
1|\|\|3871c-473
(,3|_|38710|\|8
0|=
73|V|!"0|"\4|_1
7\', |-|1870|"\\,
4|\|[]
8|_|3.|3(71\V|17
\'.0|\| 4
|=0|"\|V|4|_
|_3V3|_ 7|-
|383
|\|4|"\|"\471\V3
8 3|V|30|]\'
71|V|3
7|"\4V3|_
|=0|"\
3><4|V|!"|_3.
V14 4|3|"\|_||"7
8|"47|1|_ 4|\|[]
73|V|!"0|"\4|_
|]18|_0(4710|\|
8 1|\| 8|-
|0|"\7,
|\|4|"\|"\471\V3
8 (4|\| |33
{0|\|8|]3|"\3[]
1|V|4c-
1|\|471\V3
71|V|3 |V|4(|-
|4838 0|=
71|V|3-
7|"\4V3|_
|\|4|"\|"\471\V3
:(1} 7|-|3
3\V0|_|_|710|\|
/|_|70|"14|\|
71|V|3-
7|"\4V3|_
870|"\138 0|=
7|-|3 |_473 1 9
7|-|
(3|\|7|_||"\'
4|\|[]34|"\|_\'
2 07|-|
(3|\|7|_||"\V,(
2|7|-|3
(|_083[]-|_00|"
|"4|"\4[]0><
4|\|[]
31|\|8731|\|14|
\|
|"\3|_471V17\'
|\|4|"\|"\471\V3
8 0|= 7|-|3 1 9
2 0&-1 9 4 0
8. 4|\|[0 {3} 7|-
|3
1|\|73|"\7&><7|
_|4|_
|V|!_|!_71\V3|"
\83/|=4|_|\V|1(
|\|4|"\|"\471\V3
8.0|= 7|-|3

FEMALE BODYBUILDER: Ultimately, Khlebnikov's quest was not a delusion of grandeur but an unsentimental Modernist response to the violence of the early 20th Century. In a short 1919 memoire, he confesses that his project was to bring about universal peace, discover the reason and mechanisms that initiate andconstitute reality, and ultimately "discover the reason for all those deaths" by employing poetry, mathematics, and experimental prose to understand and engineer time and the universe as a single object.

MALE BODYBUILDER: In short, we do not get the portrait of the vigorous poet-Revolutionary of the likes of his friend Vladimir Mayakovski, but, instead, we get the portrait of an eccentric, highly sensitive poet unsentimentally attempting to make sense of immense personal and historical grief using the finer instruments of mathematics, music, and narrative. He sought to engineer the chronotopic universe via remodeling; unfortunately, he was to diefar too young to see that, with the technical word, the atomic foundations for such a mad project are now at our fingertips.

[MALE BODYBUILDER snaps fingers in beckons a BULLIED, KIDNAPPED, KNOCK KNEED POLICE OFFICER from off-stage left. FEMALE BODYBUILDER thrusts recipe cards into OFFICER's shaking hands and juts her jaw in his direction voicelessly commanding him to read]

BULLIED, KIDNAPPED, KNOCK KNEED POLICE OFFICER: *[Shakey, hesitant voice]* If today the novel is indeed dead, then let it rest. From its dusty grave rises the scintillation of unknowing and the upward velocity towards uncertain destinations. Long live the granular novel. The word too is dead. No matter - keep your face expressionless.

[MALE, BODYBUILDER, FEMALE BODYBUILDER, and BULLIED, KIDNAPPED, KNOCK KNEED POLICE OFFICER die. PLASTIC PALM TREE looks left, then right. Waddles over to MALE, BODYBUILDER, FEMALE BODYBUILDER, and BULLIED, KIDNAPPED, KNOCK KNEED POLICE OFFICER].

PLASTIC PALM TREE: *[pickpockets MALE BODYBUILDER, FEMALE*

31 4E 53 20 4F
46 20 4E 41 53
53 42 45 56 53
55 54 20 20 54
45 45 20 47 52
45 45 4B 53 20
4F 16 20 4F 44
59 53 53 35 55
53 2C 20 54 45
54 48 49 41 4E
53 20 20 56 48
45 20 42 52 4A
45 46 53 20 4C
16 20 50 15 57
19 43 46 45 52
2C 20 54 48 45
20 52 4F 4D 45
45 53 21 20 48
47 20 41 54 57
11 43 19 45 44
30 47 4E 45 20
11 41 44 39 54
19 44 48 41 4C
20 53 46 52 49
4E 47 24 20 42
15 54 52 45 48
16 20 54 42 45
20 59 45 41 52
20 37 38 2C 20
54 42 45 20 49
4E 56 51 53 49
4F 4E 20 4F 46
20 54 48 45 20
53 43 59 54 48
49 51 4E 58 20
4F 46 20 41 4E
49 41 20 53 41
48 11 3E 20 41
4E 44 20 54 48
45 20 59 45 41
52 20 31 39 38
30 20 14 54 48
45 20 45 41 53
54 3E 20 48 41
20 53 57 55 44
49 45 44 20 54
48 45 20 50 4F
53 53 49 42 49
4C 19 54 19 45
53 20 4F 46 20
50 3C 41 59 46
4E 47 20 4F 4E
20 41 4C 4C 20
52 45 45 45 4E
20 53 54 52 49
4E 17 53 2E
201D 20 20 41
54 20 54 68 49
53 20 53 4F 4E
47 20 42 39 56
45 53 20 42 4F
54 48 20 4F 41
20 41 4E 44 20
54 48 45 20 41
50 45 53 20 53
50 45 43 69 41
4C 20 49 4E 53
49 47 45 54 20
49 41 54 3E 20
54 49 4D 45 20
28 57 48 49 43
48 20 4D 45 41
4E 53 20 4C 4F
54 54 4C 45 20
54 4F 20 48 41 *

BODYBUILDER, and BULLIED, KIDNAPPED, KNOCK KNEED POLICE OFFICER. Turns to audience:] Long live the patamathematical poetry of the technical word as such. [dies]...

[CURTAIN]

\V\1773|\|133|°
\c-8|_|c-c-3878
7|-|477|-|3
{0|\|73|\|7 0|=
7|-|383
870|°\138 4|°\3
°|\|4|°\|°\471\V
3 |\/|4{|-
|1|\|38° 1|\| 4
°|\|4|°\|°\470|_
0c-1{4|_
|_4|30|°\470|°\\
"' \V\|-|3|°\3
4|_|7|-|0|°\8
4|\|[]
|°\34|]3|°\8
1|\|\V3871c-473
{J|_|38710|\|8
0|=
73|\V|1°|°\4|_|
7\'. |-|1870|°\\.
4|\|[]
8|_|[3.[3|71\V17
\'. 0|\| 4
|=0|°\|V|4|_
|_3\V3|_. 7|-
|383
|\|4|°\|°\471\V3
8 3|\V|[30[]\'
71|\V|3
7|°\4\V3|_.
|=0|°\
3><4|\V|1°|_3,
\V14 48|°\|_||°7
8|°4714|_4|\|[]
73|\V|1°0|°\4|_
[]18|_0[4710|\|
8. 1|\| 8|-
|0|°\7,
|\|4|°\|°\471\V3
8 [4|\| |33
{0|\|81[]3|°\3[]
1|\V|4c-
1|\|471\V3
71|\V|3 |\V|4{|-
|4838 0|=
71|\V|3-
7|°\4\V3|_
|\|4|°\|°\471\V3
:{1}7|-|3
3\V0|_|_|710|\|
/|_|70|°14|\|
71|\V|3-
7|°\4\V3|_
870|°\138 0|=
7|-|3 |_473 1 9
7|-|
{3|\|7|_||°\\'
4|\|[] 34|°\|_\'
2 0 7|-|
{3|\|7|_||°\\. |
2 |7|-|3
{|_083|]-|_00|°
|°4|°\4[]0><
4|\|[]
31|\|8731|\|14|
\|
|°\3|_471\V17\'
|\|4|°\|°\471\V3
8 0|= 7|-|3 1 9
2 0 8-1 9 4 0
8, 4|\|[] {3}7|-
|3
1|\|73|°\73><7|

ABOUT THE AUTHOR

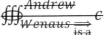 Andrew Wenaus $\Longrightarrow$ c is a

[i] Wittenberg, David. *Time Travel: the Popular Philosophy of Narrative*. (Fordham University Press, 2013).

[ii] Cooke, Raymond. *Velimir Khlebnikov: a Critical Study*. (Cambridge University Press, 1987), 71.

[iii] Ibid..

[iv] Khlebnikov, Velimir. "Ka." *The King of Time: Selected Writings of the Russian Futurian*. (Harvard University Press, 1985), 67.

[v] Ibid.

[vi] Ibid, 67-68.

[vii] Bakhtin, M. M and Michael Holquist. *The Dialogic Imagination : Four Essays*. (University of Texas Press, 1981), 425-426.

[viii] Ibid, 426.

[ix] The two significant early pieces are titled *Analogique A-B* (1957-1958). Unfortunately, both pieces were recently removed from YouTube, so I cannot link to them here. However, they are generally not difficult to find at most public and institutional libraries.

[x] Ross, Alex. *The Rest is Noise: Listening to the Twentieth Century*, (New York: Farrar, Straus and Giroux, 2007), 395.

[xi] Xenakis, Iannis. *Formalized Music: Thought and Math in Composition*, Revised Ed, (Stuyvesant, NY : Pendragon Press, 1992), 1.

[xii] An abbreviation for Unité Polyagogique Informatique CEMAMu developed by Xenakis at the *Centre d'Etudes de Mathématique et Automatique Musicales* (CEMAMu) in Paris.

[xiii] Disruption of the standard practices in film and photography were also a central concern of Dadaists and surrealists in the early-twentieth-century. For more, see Candice Black's *Ghosts of the Black Chamber: Experimental, Dada & Surrealist Photography 1918-1948*, (Solar Books, 2010).

[xiv] Roland Meyer, "Technical Images," *Flusseriana: An Intellectual Toolbox*, Edited by Siegfried Zielinski, Peter Weibel, and Daniel Irrgang, (Univocal, 2015), 388.

[xv] Siratori, Kenji. *Paracelsus* (Sweat Drenched Press, 2022), n.p.

[xvi] Siratori, Kenji. *Mind Virus* (Monstaar Media, 2008), 123.

[xvii] Siratori, Kenji. *Transcedental Machine* (Anonymous Zone, 2020). n.p.

[xviii] Siratori, Kenji. *Hack_*, (Minerva, 2011), 80.

[xix] Berardi, Franco. *Breathing: Chaos and Poetry*, (Semiotext(e), 2018), 53.

[xx] Bakhtin, Mikhail. "Epic and Novel: Toward a Methodology for the Study of the Novel." *The Dialogic Imagination: Four Essays*. Ed. Michael Holquist. Translated by Caryl Emerson and Michael Holquist (University of Texas Press, 1981), 3.

Manufactured by Amazon.ca
Acheson, AB